剑桥双语分级阅读·小说馆（第2版）

原版系列编辑 Philip Prowse

U0953650

Love in the Lakes 情定湖区

[英] 彭尼·汉考克 著
蒋菲 编译

北京语言大学出版社
BEIJING LANGUAGE AND CULTURE UNIVERSITY PRESS

CAMBRIDGE UNIVERSITY PRESS

社图号25017

北京市版权局著作权合同登记图字：01-2024-3256号

图书在版编目（CIP）数据

情定湖区 ： 英汉对照 / （英）彭尼·汉考克（Penny Hancock）著 ； 蒋菲编译. -- 2版. -- 北京 ： 北京语言大学出版社, 2025. 3. --（剑桥双语分级阅读小说馆）. -- ISBN 978-7-5619-6736-2

Ⅰ. H319.4

中国国家版本馆CIP数据核字第20256DU094号

情定湖区
QING DING HUQU

责任编辑： 李　珍
责任印制： 周　燚

出版发行： 北京语言大学出版社
社　　址： 北京市海淀区学院路 15 号，100083
网　　址： www.blcup.com
电子信箱： service@blcup.com
电　　话： 编 辑 部 010-8230 1019
发 行 部 010-8230 3650/3591/3648
北语书店 010-8230 3653
网购咨询 010-8230 3908
印　　刷： 东港股份有限公司

版　　次： 2017 年 6 月第 1 版　2025 年 3 月第 2 版
印　　次： 2025 年 3 月第 1 次印刷
开　　本： 880 毫米 × 1230 毫米　1/32
印　　张： 6.625
字　　数： 156 千字
定　　价： 23.00 元

PRINTED IN CHINA
凡有印装质量问题，本社负责调换。售后QQ号1367565611，电话010-82303590

Preface

前言

“剑桥双语分级阅读·小说馆”是一套从剑桥大学出版社引进的面向非英语国家英语学习者的分级系列读物，由英语语言教学专家及小说作家合力创作。创作过程历时三十余年，出版后受到世界各地英语教师和英语学习者的喜爱，许多读本再版多次，三十余年来畅销不衰，成为受全球英语学习者青睐的优秀读本。

本系列读物具有以下突出特色：

1. 是原创英语读物，而非改编自普通作品的读物。因此，阅读本系列读物，我们读到的是原汁原味的原创英语，而非人为改编过的二手英语。

2. 是当代优秀短篇小说，而非年代久远的小说。因此，阅读本系列读物，我们读到的是当今鲜活的、学了就能用的英语，而非穿越时空的、学了用不上的英语；了解的是与读者同时代不同国家人们的生活和思想，而非隔代人的生活、文化和风土人情。

3. 是专为非英语国家的英语学习者量身定制的读物，而非为英语母语者所写的大众读物。因此，本系列读物是中国读者首选的英语学习读物。

4. 是英美知名小说家和英语语言教学专家合力创作的读物。小说家保障了读物的可读性与可欣赏性，英语语言教学专家保障了读物语言作为英语习得材料的科学性与可学性。

本系列读物中的多个读本都曾在世界上颇具影响力的“语言学习者文学奖”（Language Learner Literature Award）评选中获得大奖。因此，阅读本系列读物，我们会在欣赏小说的同时，自然而然地、有效地提高自己的英语水平。

5. 本系列读物的故事题材丰富多样，包括侦探、情感、历险、悬疑、人文、科幻、喜剧等，读者可以随心选择自己喜欢的类别阅读；故事内容生动有趣，故事情节引人入胜、扣人心弦，读者一旦开始阅读，就想一口气读完，使阅读真正升华到“悦读”。

6. 随书附赠的音频材料内容精彩，是专业配音员的演绎再创作。听着它，我们犹如在听广播剧、听评书，又仿佛是在听电影、听话剧……这种聆听英语的享受将彻底扫除学生对英语听力的畏难心理。

7. 本系列读物所使用的语言，既有英式英语，也有美式英语，对应的音频材料也相应分为英音和美音，读者可根据自己的喜好来选择。

8. 本系列近百本读物根据《欧洲语言共同参考框架》（CEFR）和剑桥大学外语考评部开发的 ESOL 考试的标准来确定级别划分，是建立在科学研究和实践基础之上的分级。全套共分七个级别（与中国学生英语基础水平的大致对应关系，请参见图书封底表格），读者可根据自己的英语基础选择相应级别的读本来学习。

为了更好地帮助中国学生学习和欣赏，“剑桥双语分级阅读·小说馆”从剑桥大学出版社原版引进后又增加了以下内容：

1. 增加了适量的辅助学习内容，包括“读前思考”“读后活动”“学习指导”三个板块，其中“学习指导”板块又包括生词、短语和表达、文化点滴、阅读练习四项内容。增加这些板块的目的是全方位帮助学生提升英语阅读能力，扩充词汇量，扫除阅读中的文化障碍，增强对英语小说的鉴赏能力。

2. 增加了小说全文的参考译文。出于语言学习的考虑，译文多采用直译，但也尽量符合中文的表达习惯。

值得一提的是，所增加的辅助学习内容和参考译文，全部由来自全国不同省市知名中学（包括人大附中、北大附中、清华附中、黄冈中学、上海中学等三十余所中学）的一线英语教师完成。这些一线教师的加盟，确保了所加内容与中国学生的英语学习特点和学习需求相吻合，为学生阅读和欣赏读物、提高英语水平给予恰到好处的助力。

英语阅读是英语课堂的延伸和补充，也是培养英语语感、提高英语水平的有效途径。选择一套好的英语读物，收获的将不仅仅是语言的进步。欢迎年轻朋友们来到“剑桥双语分级阅读·小说馆”，打开一本本好书，品味一个个好故事，为实现梦想搭建桥梁。

北京语言大学出版社

Contents 目录

People in the story

故事中的人物

Robert: a vet who lives in the Lake District

罗伯特：居住在湖区的一名兽医

Laura: the owner of a food shop and café in London

劳拉：伦敦一家食品店兼咖啡馆的主人

Joseph: Laura's neighbour

约瑟夫：劳拉的邻居

Nick: Laura's boyfriend

尼克：劳拉的男朋友

Maggie: Robert's receptionist

玛吉：罗伯特的接待员

Barbara: Robert's aunt

芭芭拉：罗伯特的姑妈

Jo: working with Laura in London

乔：劳拉在伦敦的同事

A farmer

一个农民

Before reading
读前思考

1. Look at the title and the picture on the front cover. What kind of story do you think it is going to be?
2. If you have the recording, listen to Chapter 1.

Chapter 1
The Lakes

There was a crash. A long, loud scream. Then silence.

Robert heard the crash and the scream as he came out of the woods and drove past the lake. Every day he hoped that he would get past the lake without it happening. But here it was again. The sound of an ambulance. Blue lights going on and off. He began to shake in fear. To his left, out of the corner of his eye, he could see that the water was red with blood.

He stopped the car. He was still shaking. He put his head in his hands. When he looked up across the lake, there was nothing. There never was.

'So why, why can't I drive past this place without the same thing happening again and again?' he wondered angrily.

When he was calm again, he started driving, slowly, towards the pub.

Robert often stopped there on his way home. It was easier than cooking for himself after a long day at work. The pub food was good, local and organic.

But the real reason Robert preferred to eat at the pub was that it meant less time in his house, the house that was silent now.

This evening he wanted to go to bed early. He was a vet and he was on call. He hoped to get as much sleep as possible before the telephone rang. There were some nights at this time of year when he didn't get woken up, it was true, but often someone wanted him. Perhaps there was a sick sheep or cow. In the spring the phone never stopped ringing. Sheep were having lambs and he was up all night. Those were the important calls – from working farmers who needed their animals. There were some people who phoned, however, when it wasn't really necessary.

For example, the other day Mrs Fellows had phoned Robert at midnight because her cat, Harry, was sneezing. It wasn't really an emergency, but Mrs Fellows was worried. So Robert got up and went to the surgery.

Robert told Mrs Fellows that Harry only had a cold and was perfectly healthy. But Mrs Fellows talked about the cat until past one o'clock. Robert nodded, but he was thinking, 'This isn't really about your cat. It's about you, Mrs Fellows.'

He didn't say anything. He understood that Mrs Fellows was lonely. It was Mrs Fellows who needed him, not the cat.

Local people thought of Robert as a kind man who always listened. These days he no longer spoke very much, but that didn't matter. They liked his quiet face, and the time he gave them. They called him 'the silent animal doctor'. They wondered about his private life, but nobody asked.

Now, Robert drove away from the lake, and put his foot down as he reached the straight road through the woods. He didn't often meet another car at this time of year. The tourists had mostly gone, and all the locals were at home by now on a September evening. He came out of the woods and tried to think about the good food that was waiting for him. He tried not to think about the lake, or the jet-skiers, or the water slowly turning red as the sun went down.

Chapter 2 London

Bang, bang, bang! Bang, bang, bang!

Laura opened her eyes. Blue lights flashed on and off outside her window. She sat up, feeling alarmed. It was still dark. Someone was banging loudly on her door.

She put on her bedside light and looked at the clock. It was two o'clock in the morning. Who was knocking on her door at this time?

She pulled on a dressing gown and slippers and ran to open the front door. An ambulance driver was standing there.

'I'm sorry to wake you at this time of night,' he said.

'What... Who...?' Laura couldn't speak. Her heart was beating fast.

'Your neighbour, Joseph Donaldson – we're taking him to hospital. We think he's had a heart attack,' the ambulance driver said.

'Oh no! Can I do anything to help?' asked Laura.

Joseph was the old man next door. Laura liked

him very much and she often helped him. But he was old. He'd had a bad heart for a long time. She had to admit that she was thankful it was Joseph, and not one of her own family or friends who was ill.

'Well, yes,' said the ambulance driver, 'that's what I'm here to ask. It's about his dog. Joseph says you offered to care for the dog if anything ever happened to him. He wants you to take the dog while he goes into hospital.'

'Oh, OK. I'll come,' said Laura.

A few minutes later Laura was standing in Joseph's sitting room, holding a small dog in her arms. She watched the ambulance people carry Joseph out.

The old man looked up at Laura.

'You will take care of him, won't you?' he said. Laura took Joseph's hand.

'Don't you worry,' she said. 'I'll look after him, I promise.'

'Because I don't want Kip to die before me,' said the old man.

'Oh no, I'm sure he won't,' said Laura kindly, then suddenly wondered if that was the right thing to say.

'I mean...' she went on. 'Look, neither of you are going to die. You're going to be fine, and I'll keep Kip until you come home.'

'Thank you, my dear. You're a good girl,' said Joseph, and he was gone.

The ambulance drove away and Laura watched it go with the little dog in her arms.

Then she remembered. 'I'm going away to the Lake District this afternoon with Nick! What's he going to say about this dog?' she thought.

She remembered what Nick had said to her. 'I usually go alone. I like to get back to the earth, do a bit of water sports and so on. But I don't want to spend four days away from you. If, that is, you'd like to come?'

And Laura had said, 'Yes! Yes, of course I'd like to come!'

Four days in the Lakes! And with Nick!

She'd only met him a few weeks ago. He'd come into her shop and café for a cappuccino one day. Then he'd come in the next day and the day after that, and Laura had begun to wonder who this smart, funny man was.

She and her assistant in the shop, Jo, often played guessing games about their customers. They guessed their names, their jobs, what they were like. It was a good way of passing the time when the shop was quiet and it made them laugh.

'What do you think he does?' Laura asked Jo one day.

Nick had just left the shop. He was wearing a leather jacket and a smart, Paul Smith shirt.

'I think he's a bank manager,' said Jo.

'Oh no!' said Laura. 'He's more arty than that.'

'A fashion designer?' suggested Jo.

'No, I think he's probably a people person – a teacher maybe?' said Laura.

'Too smart! A doctor?' said Jo.

'No, too relaxed-looking. Perhaps he's a film director?' said Laura.

'Yes, a film director called Francesco!' Jo laughed.

'Miles,' said Laura.

'OK, Miles,' agreed Jo. 'He directs thrillers and in his free time he goes rock climbing. And he likes you, Laura.'

'Hmm,' Laura said. 'I quite like the idea of a rock-climbing film director!' Jo and Laura both laughed.

At last Nick asked Laura out. He worked near Laura's café he said, as a designer. He lived in a smart new flat. He rode a motorbike and he owned a sports car. He liked going motor racing, he told Laura.

'Not rock climbing?' Laura asked him, her eyes shining.

'No, I don't like heights,' answered Nick. 'Why do you ask?'

'It doesn't matter,' she said. 'I was just wondering.'

They started to see each other regularly. Laura enjoyed being with him. They went to good restaurants and pubs beside the river Thames, and he told her stories that made her laugh.

And now he'd asked her to go away with him, to the Lake District. One of her favourite places in England. One of the best places for walking in England. So he wasn't just a city type, he liked the countryside too! And that mattered to Laura. It mattered a lot.

As she got back into bed, with Kip lying on the end of it, Laura felt confused.

'If Nick doesn't want the dog to go, perhaps I'll have to stay here,' she thought. 'I promised Joseph I'd look after Kip and I can't let him down.'

She thought of four days alone in her flat with a dog. She thought of being with Nick in the Lakes. She knew which she would prefer. She loved the countryside. And maybe...maybe she was beginning to love Nick. She wasn't sure. It was a long time since she had liked, really liked, anyone.

'OK.' She smiled to herself. 'He is not a film director after all. But he is clever and funny and I do enjoy being with him...and I do want to go away with him. So what's he going to say about the dog?'

Chapter 3
The dog comes too

'A dog?' he asked.

'Yes, a dog!'

'That dog?'

'Yes, this dog.'

It was four o'clock on Thursday afternoon. Nick had arrived at Laura's flat in his sports car. They'd both agreed to take Friday off work.

Laura stood in the open door. In her arms was a small dog. It had long ears and long hair. It was the colour of that nice paint Nick had just redone his flat with. The paint was called 'Bone'.

'We're not taking a dog to the Lake District!' said Nick.

'I'm sorry,' said Laura. 'Joseph went into hospital last night. He had a heart attack. So I've got to look after the dog. I'm afraid if he can't come with us, I can't come at all.'

'Joseph? Who's Joseph?' asked Nick.

'You know, he's the old man I told you about. He's my neighbour – my friend,' explained Laura.

'Oh, him!' Nick remembered now. Laura often

talked about an old man who she sometimes visited. Nick hadn't listened very carefully. After all, the man was seventy-six. Nick wasn't very interested in seventy-six-year-old men.

'Hasn't he got anyone else he can ask?' suggested Nick.

'No, Nick,' said Laura. 'You remember, I told you his wife died last year. There's nobody else to look after the dog.'

'Hasn't he got children...grandchildren?' Nick went on.

'No, he's only got me,' said Laura.

Nick made a 'tut' sound with his tongue. He'd been looking forward to a weekend away jet-skiing on the lakes. Then he'd decided to ask Laura along. He never usually invited his girlfriends away with him.

And now she was bringing a dog! Normally he would be very annoyed. But as he looked at Laura, with her wild blonde hair and her pink cheeks, holding the little dog in her arms, he couldn't help thinking how attractive she looked.

'You,' said Nick, walking round behind Laura now and kissing her hair, 'are too kind. That's your problem. So we're taking a dog on holiday with us... Well, it'll be...interesting, I suppose.'

Laura smiled at him. 'You mean Kip *can* come too?'

'Only because if he doesn't, you won't. And I want you with me,' said Nick.

'Oh, that's wonderful! I was so looking forward to this weekend!' said Laura.

'Good. Well, let's get going,' said Nick. 'Are your bags packed?'

'All ready,' said Laura pointing to two bags beside the front door.

'Now, where are we going to put the dog?' asked Nick.

'He can sit with me,' suggested Laura.

'Is that allowed? He'll have to go in the back, on top of the luggage,' said Nick.

* * *

'I think we need to stop,' said Laura.

It was four hours later. Nick and Laura had left London and were driving north.

'What?' asked Nick.

'Nick, we must stop! Kip needs to get out,' said Laura.

Kip was sitting on top of their luggage. The small sports car was full. There were Laura's two bags, Nick's expensive leather suitcase and his wetsuits.

The dog was barking now. Nick looked annoyed.

'Nick, I'm thinking of your luggage,' said Laura.

'OK, OK,' said Nick. He parked the car at the side of the road, but it was clear he wasn't happy about stopping for a dog.

'It's going to be midnight by the time we get there,' he said.

'I'm sorry,' said Laura when she came back to the car with Kip.

If this dog stopped her getting to know Nick better, she would be so unhappy. But what could she do? She had to help poor old Joseph.

She gave Nick a quick look as they set off again. Was he angry with her? He looked back at her and smiled. He took hold of her hand and held it. And she relaxed.

'Everything's going to be all right,' she thought. 'Perhaps Nick will even learn to love this little dog.'

* * *

An hour and a half later Nick slowed down outside a pub.

'Why are we stopping?' asked Laura.

'We need to eat. We're nearly there now and I'm really hungry!'

'But I've got food in my bag. I brought some things from my shop. I can cook when we arrive.'

Laura felt disappointed. Cooking was her great love. She'd been looking forward to cooking for Nick this weekend. And while she was here in the Lakes, she wanted to find good, local food for their other meals.

'I'm just not sure what the kitchen is like,' Nick said. Laura thought he looked rather guilty.

'What do you mean?' she asked.

'It's just that the kitchen may not be very modern,' replied Nick. 'Anyway I want to buy you dinner. You've been working all week. You've earned it.'

The pub where they stopped for food was warm and welcoming, though it was almost empty.

Laura and Nick sat in a corner near the fire. There were flowers on their table. The pub smelt of wood smoke and good food. They studied the menu and chose their meals.

'Not bad,' said Laura, eating a piece of chicken pie and salad. She enjoyed tasting local food everywhere she went. She was always keeping an eye open for new things to sell in her café. Nick was eating pheasant.

'It's good that it's organic, local food, don't you think?' said Laura.

'Yeah, but I could do with a good Thai green curry,' said Nick, and Laura hit him playfully.

Kip sat under the table. Laura fed him bits of

chicken.

At the bar sat a tall man with untidy fair hair. Laura looked at him. He was interesting-looking, she thought, with an intelligent face. But he looked sad.

What would Jo say about him? A poet, she might guess. A hill-walking poet, like Wordsworth?

The man didn't look at the couple, although they were the only other people in the room. If anything, Laura noticed, he seemed to turn away from them.

'They aren't very friendly around here,' said Nick. 'I thought Northerners were always friendly.'

'Well, it's just one person,' said Laura. 'You can't make up your mind about all Northerners because of one person's behaviour.'

'But there's nobody else here. Why doesn't he say hello?'

'Maybe he doesn't like tourists,' said Laura, beginning to build up a picture of the man in her head. She could see him walking across the hills in the rain, then going home to a tiny house and writing sad poems by the light of a fire. He was probably quite poor. Writers never earned much money.

'Do you think he's a poet?' she asked Nick.

'Who?' asked Nick.

'That man at the bar,' said Laura.

'A poet? I've no idea,' said Nick. 'He looks very unfriendly. That's all I can see. Why do you ask?'

'Oh, never mind,' said Laura. 'Look, I'm tired,' she

said. 'Shall we get to the house?'

'House?' repeated Nick.

'The place where we're staying,' said Laura.

'Oh, that! Yes, let's go,' replied Nick.

Chapter 4
Poison!

'A barn? A farm building?' asked Laura.

'Yes, a barn!' replied Nick.

'But...but I thought you were a hot-bath and soft-towels sort of a man,' said Laura.

'Yes, I am, when I'm in London,' replied Nick. 'But when I'm in the country I like to live the country way.'

'Are you saying that country people all live in cold barns?' asked Laura, laughing.

'I'm saying that it's good for a man to give up his comfortable city life sometimes.'

'It may be good for men,' said Laura, 'but I'm not so sure it's good for this woman, or this poor little dog!'

They'd parked the car outside the door of a large, stone building. It was eleven o'clock at night and Laura couldn't believe her eyes as they pushed open the door. They might just as well be camping! There were lights, but not much else. No heating. No TV. No bath. There was a tiny kitchen with a camping stove to cook on. And at the top of some wooden stairs

there were beds. It was cold.

Kip ran off across the big room into a smaller side room. Laura went into the kitchen.

'Nick, why didn't you tell me we were staying in a barn?' asked Laura.

'Because,' he said, putting his arms around her, 'I was afraid, if I told you, that you wouldn't come.'

'Well, you were right!' said Laura.

Nick laughed. 'But you're here now,' he said, 'and it's a long way home.'

Laura laughed too and let him pull her towards him. 'So you tricked me,' she said, 'into coming with you.'

'And you tricked me into bringing a dog with us,' he replied.

'Yes,' she said, smiling. He kissed her.

'I'd better just check on Kip,' said Laura.

Nick pretended to look hurt. 'I hope you don't start liking that dog more than you like me!' he said.

'Hey!' said Laura. 'You're not a helpless motherless animal! I'll just go and see...'

'You'll need a torch,' said Nick. 'There's no electricity in that room. Here you are.'

Laura went across the cold barn. She was

surprised that Nick had chosen this barn for the holiday. He didn't seem like the kind of man to enjoy camping – it was interesting what people showed about themselves, the more you got to know them. But she felt happy. It showed he was even more interesting than she'd thought. And although she'd joked with Nick, Laura did in fact love camping. She loved the idea of cooking on a camping stove. She loved sitting by a real fire to keep warm! 'I'm a country girl at heart,' she thought. 'So, Nick and I are more alike than I imagined!'

She pulled her wool jacket around herself and went towards the side room holding the torch. She opened the door and shone the torch around the room. No Kip!

There was a door to the garden. Laura realised it wasn't shut properly. Had Kip gone out? She pushed the door open.

'Kip! Kip!' she called. She went outside and shone her torch about. It lit up the bushes and trees.

Laura's heart began to beat fast. She walked further out into the trees.

'Kip! Kip! Where are you?' she called. She began to feel worried. Perhaps he was lost. Perhaps a bigger

animal had eaten him. Did foxes eat dogs? She had no idea.

What had happened to Kip? What would she do if she'd lost him? If Joseph knew something bad had happened to Kip, he'd be heartbroken and might not get better! She knew how much he loved his little dog.

She stood in the trees for several minutes calling, 'Kip! Kip!' but there was no sound.

'I'd better go back,' thought Laura. 'Nick will wonder where I am.' She turned back towards the barn.

'Laura! Laura! Where are you?' Nick was calling her.

'Out here. Looking for Kip,' she called back.

'He's here!' shouted Nick.

Laura moved as quickly as she could back through the trees. Nick stood by the door holding another torch.

'He was under the chair,' he said as Laura got back, 'but I think there may be something wrong with him.'

Laura bent down and touched the little dog. He didn't move or open his eyes.

'Hey, look! What's this?' asked Nick. His light was shining on some powder in an open box on the floor.

'What is it?' asked Laura, picking up the box.

Her heart jumped. On the box it said, 'Rat Poison'.

'Oh no! Nick, has he eaten it?' cried Laura.

'It looks like he's got the powder round his mouth,' replied Nick.

'Oh! What shall we do?' cried Laura.

'There isn't much we can do,' said Nick.

'I promised Joseph. I *promised* Joseph I would take care of him. Will he die, Nick?' said Laura.

'I've no idea,' said Nick.

'But if Kip dies, Joseph might die... Look, we need to get him to a vet,' said Laura.

'Laura, it's nearly midnight!' said Nick.

'There must be emergency vets, like there are emergency doctors,' said Laura.

She was holding Kip on her knees. He looked very ill.

'Laura,' said Nick, 'we've only got four nights here alone together. I'm not spending one of them looking for a vet for an animal that isn't even ours!'

'I mustn't disappoint Joseph,' said Laura. She put her hand on the dog's side again. He felt cool.

'He's terribly ill,' she said, really frightened now. 'And it's my fault. We must do something!'

Laura looked at Nick. Why didn't he understand that she didn't *want* to do this, she *had* to? She had to do it because she'd promised Joseph.

Nick looked annoyed. 'I'm going to bed,' he said. 'I'm tired after the drive and I want to get up early tomorrow.'

Nick went upstairs, leaving Laura alone with Kip in her arms. She was near to tears. But were they tears of worry for the dog or disappointment with Nick? She wasn't sure.

Chapter 5 Emergency call-out

Another crash. A scream. Lights going on and off. Blood on the water.

Robert woke up. His heart was beating wildly, but the house was dark. It was the dream again. The same dream every night. The dream was like living that terrible night over and over again. Yet it was two whole years ago now. Why wouldn't it stop?

He sat up and looked at the clock. Midnight. After a few seconds, he realised the phone was ringing. He picked it up.

'Emergency. A poisoned dog,' a voice said. It was his emergency phone centre.

Robert wrote down a name, still half asleep. He put on his trousers and a big pullover, and set off to the surgery.

Often, the emergency calls came from people with pets that had nothing wrong with them, like Mrs Fellows' cat. Robert liked animals. But animals

had different needs to people. They didn't need a vet every time they had a cold.

The worst people, Robert thought as he drove along, were the city people who came for holidays in the summer. They came with their ugly, bright-coloured clothes, and filled the lakes with their noisy water sports. Often, they brought dogs or even cats with them. Sometimes the dogs ran after the sheep on the hills. Farmers got angry about that.

But the real reason Robert disliked people from the city was more painful and he refused to talk about it.

There were no other cars on the road. He tried not to think of that evening two years ago as he drove. He needed to stay calm.

It took him ten minutes to get to his surgery. He jumped out of the car, opened the surgery door and put on the lights. He put some clean paper on the table and got some things ready. A poisoned dog. That was all he knew.

* * *

Laura didn't like driving alone along the dark roads at this time of night. But although she'd asked Nick again if he would come with her, he'd refused.

'Take the car if you like,' he'd said, 'but I need my sleep. It's up to you. You can stay here with me or take the dog to the vet. But I'm not going anywhere.'

She felt afraid as she drove along the empty, dark country roads, past the lake, then through some woods and up another hill, following – she hoped – the directions she'd been given on the phone.

She wished Nick was with her. She'd felt disappointed with him earlier, but now she thought about it differently as she drove.

'He said he didn't usually bring anyone to the Lakes with him,' she thought. 'He certainly didn't expect me to bring a dog. He doesn't want to spend all night looking for a vet. It isn't really surprising.'

It was nearly one o'clock when she stopped outside a small building. 'Veterinary Surgery' was written clearly above it. A light shone from inside, so she knew this must be the right place.

Kip was on the front seat of the car, covered with her jumper and coat to keep him warm. Laura lifted his little body out of the car, hurried to the door and rang the doorbell. The door opened.

Laura wasn't sure what she'd been expecting. Probably someone middle-aged, with grey hair and

glasses. Instead, she recognised at once the man who'd been in the pub earlier that evening and thought, stupidly, 'But you're the poet!'

He was dressed in an old jumper and his fair hair was unbrushed. So, a vet, not a poet! Her guess had been very wide of the mark! If Kip hadn't been so ill, she might have smiled.

'You think he's been poisoned?' the vet asked, taking Kip from Laura.

'Yes, there was rat poison on the floor in the room where I left him,' said Laura.

'Did you bring some with you?' the vet asked.

'No,' replied Laura.

'And you didn't check the room before you left the dog in it?' the vet asked.

'No. We'd just arrived. It was a six-hour drive from London. I was tired, I didn't think...I didn't think there would be rat poison on the floor,' said Laura.

'Where are you staying?' the vet asked.

'We're camping...' Laura told him.

'You're camping?' the vet said.

'Well, it's sort of camping – in a barn,' explained Laura.

'Camping in a barn?' the vet said.

Laura wished he wouldn't keep repeating everything she said. It made her feel so stupid. And he still hadn't smiled. His hair covered most of his face anyway, so she had no idea what he was thinking.

He was silent then, for what seemed like a long, long time.

Robert didn't speak. He felt annoyed. 'This is what they're like,' he thought. 'The people who come to the Lakes have no idea how to live in the country. You stay in a barn – so you don't want rats. Of course there'll be rat poison, and if you've got a dog, you check the place first.'

Laura watched. His big hands felt the dog's little chest, its tummy and picked up each of its ears in turn. He smelled the ears.

'Where is this place you're staying?' he asked.

'It's up on Bakestall Fell. It's like a...well, it's just a barn with some beds. It's pretty cold and there are obviously rats, but...' She realised he wasn't really listening.

'I need to give the dog some medicine,' he said.

'Will he be all right?' asked Laura.

'I think we're probably just in time,' the vet replied. He gave her a quick look. 'You were right to

phone me. He could have died.'

While the vet gave the dog the medicine, Laura sat and watched. 'Why didn't I check the barn for poison?' she thought. 'But I'm not used to having a dog. I didn't think about Kip's safety.'

She watched the vet, his large hands working so gently on the dog. His face, although unsmiling, was a gentle face, she thought. But she noticed again that there was something deeply sad about him.

Kip's eyes were open now, and he looked a little better.

'It's a barn, you say. Is there any heating? Any hot water?' the vet asked.

'No, it's very basic,' Laura replied.

'Then, look,' he said. At last he stood up straight and looked at her, pushing the hair away from his eyes, which, she saw now, were blue. 'I'll take the dog back to my place tonight. It'll be better for him to be warm.'

Laura was surprised. Surprised and so thankful she wanted to kiss him. It seemed so kind – kinder than was necessary. But she could see that he wasn't the type of man you could kiss, however thankful you felt.

'Thank you,' she said instead. 'Thank you so much. You must think I'm stupid not checking the barn first, but...'

'I'll bring him back to you tomorrow. What's the address?' the vet asked.

Laura told the vet where the barn was and he nodded.

'I know it,' he said. 'I'm going out there anyway tomorrow to see a farmer. I'll bring the dog back in the morning, if he's better.'

'That's so good of you,' replied Laura. 'I feel so much better. I was worried and I didn't know what to do.'

Laura felt happy at last. Kip was going to be all right. She turned to go.

'Um...' The vet spoke just as she stepped out of the door. She turned round.

'I forgot to ask – what's his name?' the vet said.

'Whose name?' asked Laura.

The vet looked at her as if she was mad, then touched the dog's head.

'Oh...oh sorry,' said Laura. 'It's Kip.'

'Right. Good night,' he said.

And Laura set off again through the night feeling much better than she'd felt on the way there.

Chapter 6
On the lake

In the morning Nick came into the kitchen. Laura was cooking bacon on the tiny camping stove.

'That smells good,' he said.

'Here.' Laura handed him a plate. 'Perhaps we can go for a walk together before Nick goes off to do his water sports,' she was thinking.

Nick had other ideas. He ate his breakfast quickly, before Laura sat down.

'Right!' he said loudly. 'I feel better for that. Now, let's get going!'

'Already?' Laura asked.

'I don't want to waste any time,' said Nick. 'It's a beautiful morning and I want to get out on the lake while it's fine. Are you coming?'

'I'm...I'm not sure. What water sports are you doing? I quite like sailing, but I don't know if...'

'Jet-skiing,' said Nick.

'Jet-skiing?' Laura looked at him. Why was she surprised? Nick liked fast vehicles. He liked motorbikes and sports cars, so of course he liked jet-skiing.

'Coming?' he asked.

'No, no, I don't think so. I've never jet-skied. To be honest, I'm a bit afraid of it. You have to go so fast.'

'That's the fun!' said Nick. 'But don't worry. I'm happy to go on my own, and I can meet you back here for lunch.'

'OK. I'll come with you down to the lake, and walk back. I need some exercise too,' said Laura.

Nick hadn't asked about Kip. He'd been asleep when Laura had got back last night. Had he forgotten that she'd gone to the vet's in the middle of the night?

'The vet kept the dog overnight,' Laura said as they drove. 'He was worried he'd be cold in the barn.'

'That was kind of him,' said Nick. 'So, he was all right?'

'Yes, he was OK, a bit quiet,' replied Laura.

'No, I meant the dog,' said Nick laughing.

'Oh! Oh yes, Kip was OK. But it was lucky I went. The vet said he nearly died.'

'Hey, just look at that,' said Nick, not answering Laura. A bright yellow jet-ski was racing over the water, the sun behind it. 'That's going to be me soon!'

'Cool,' said Laura, suddenly realising how little

interest she really had in jet-skis.

As they drove down the little roads – the same ones she'd gone down late last night – she thought how beautiful the countryside was. Tall hills rose on either side, lovely purple and red colours in the September sunshine, and the road turned towards the sheet of silver water that was the lake. Laura couldn't help thinking that the jet-skis on the lake were the only things that weren't beautiful.

At the water sports centre, Nick jumped out of the car and went to talk to someone.

Laura sat wondering why she was there. It was almost as if Nick had forgotten her now he was about to do the thing he loved so much – get onto a jet-ski. But to be fair, he'd told her he didn't usually invite his girlfriends. Perhaps this was why. He knew he would be busy.

'I'll just have to do things that I enjoy,' she thought.

'See you at lunchtime,' Nick said, coming back to the car.

'OK,' she said. 'I'll make lunch for you. I'll see you later.'

She didn't know why she felt disappointed. What

had she expected? That they would spend the whole weekend sitting in cafés being romantic?

'No,' she thought. 'I knew it wouldn't be like that. But it would be nice to spend some time walking together. It's such a beautiful morning.'

She walked back along the quiet roads, thinking that this was the second time she'd gone along them alone since they'd arrived.

The fields were full of mushrooms, white in the morning light. She thought about picking some to make a really good mushroom omelette for lunch.

She went back to the barn, got a large bowl and set off up the nearest hill, picking mushrooms. She could listen out for the vet's car if she stayed near the barn.

'I hope Kip's all right,' she thought. 'I'll feel happier when he's back with me again.'

The smell of the countryside and the fresh air reminded her of being a child. She'd grown up in the countryside and often missed it. However, there just weren't the same opportunities in the country as there were in London. Her shop and café were going well and she couldn't leave them now.

'I wonder if I could be happy living somewhere

like this again?' she thought as she walked.

Then she realised that something wasn't right. The peace of the countryside was being broken. It was the annoying sound of jet-skis going round and round out on the lake.

* * *

Maggie, the vet's receptionist, was sitting by her desk, looking in a small mirror and checking her make-up.

'Oh, what a little darling!' she cried, seeing the dog in Robert's arms.

'Ah, he's lovely! Whose is it? Who's your lucky mummy?' she asked, putting her hand on Kip's head. She looked up at Robert then.

'Are you coming to the White Bull later?' she asked him.

'Sorry, Maggie,' said Robert.

She smiled sweetly at him, hoping he would notice her long eyelashes.

'You need to get out more, you know,' she said. 'You're getting boring. You'll become a boring old man if you're not careful.'

Robert looked at his receptionist and gave her a quick smile. She was kind, she really was. And attractive. And she knew it! But he didn't want to spend an evening with Maggie while she talked about every pet that came into the surgery. She said he was getting boring, but she wasn't the most interesting company herself.

'I'm going out now,' he told Maggie. 'I've got to look at some cows up at Farmer Ainsworth's and I'll take this dog back to its owner on the way.'

Robert climbed into his Land Rover. He looked down at Kip on the seat beside him. He had to admit he quite liked this type of dog. Since Chiara had gone, he often felt lonely, but there was no way he could begin to share his life with another person. It would be too painful. Perhaps a dog instead? He thought about the farms around here. They didn't need more dogs running about, worrying the sheep. The thoughts ran around his head as he drove towards the barn.

Kip had his front feet up against the window and was looking out. Suddenly he saw a rabbit in a field and jumped up and down, barking loudly. No, it would be difficult having a dog with him while he tried to work.

As Robert arrived at the barn, he saw that there

was no car there. 'I don't believe it! She's gone out! She expects me to leave the dog in an empty barn,' he thought.

He got out of the Land Rover and shut the door. He walked up to the door of the barn. As he thought, it was locked. There was nobody in.

'I told that woman I'd come today,' he thought. 'Where is she? She didn't seem like the kind of woman to just forget about her dog. She seemed so worried about it!'

He walked once more around the barn, just to make sure there was nobody there. Then he remembered she said they'd come from London. He felt so annoyed he began to shake.

'She probably leaves the poor dog on its own every day in a small flat while she goes out to work,' he thought. 'It's normal for her to do this! She just has a dog because it's fashionable.'

For some reason, he felt disappointed as well as annoyed with the woman. He turned the Land Rover round and drove back down the road, with Kip still beside him.

'I'll go to Farmer Ainsworth's and come back later,' he thought.

He saw the yellow sports car as he was about to drive onto the main road. He recognised it as the car the woman had driven last night. It was parked beside the lake. And out on the lake he could see jet-skiers racing round and round, making silver patterns on the water. The skiers hadn't seen him. It would be impossible to hear a car, with all that noise. They were racing over the water, then turning suddenly so that they jumped into the air. Robert felt anger, anger that was almost like a pain in his body.

He realised one of the jet-skiers must be the owner of the car. So Kip's owner was out there jet-skiing instead of waiting at the barn for her dog! He felt the strange disappointment again.

'What sort of woman is more interested in jet-skiing than her own dog's health?' he thought.

He set off towards Farmer Ainsworth's still feeling angry. Why were jet-skiers still allowed on the lake? Nothing made him more angry and unhappy than the danger these people brought to the Lakes.

Chapter 7
Angry words

Laura collected enough mushrooms to make a good omelette. There were blackberries in the field as well and she picked some of these too. Back at the barn, she made a salad, cut up some ham and salami, and opened a jar of olives.

She put plates and glasses on the table ready for Nick when he returned from his jet-skiing.

She looked at her watch. It was nearly two o'clock! Laura couldn't believe it. Hadn't the vet said he would bring Kip back this morning?

Laura began to feel worried again. What if Kip hadn't got better after all? What if the poison had really hurt him?

When she heard the sound of a car coming, she hurried outside to see if it was the vet. She walked towards the gate and saw that it was Nick, racing up in the sports car.

He jumped out. 'That was wonderful!' he said. 'And I'm so hungry. Look, honey, I want to go water-skiing this afternoon. I met a man down there with a boat

and skis, so I'll just eat a quick lunch and then I'll go. Are you OK?'

'I'm fine,' said Laura showing him the lunch she'd made. 'But I don't know where Kip is. The vet said he'd bring him back this morning. I hope he's all right.'

Nick sat and ate the food that was on the table. Then, with his mouth full, he went towards the door.

'Hey!' said Laura. 'I'm making an omelette...'

'An omelette?' Nick said. 'It's OK. I don't want anything else now. I'll be back about six o'clock. We can go back to that pub for supper. You don't need to cook.'

He stopped outside the door and walked back inside to Laura.

'Hey!' he said. 'Give us a kiss.'

Laura stood at the door and watched him disappear again in the sports car.

She turned back to the table, which was covered with good things to eat. She looked at the pile of mushrooms all ready to go in the omelette.

'What am I going to do with all this food?' she wondered. 'And what shall I do with the rest of the afternoon? What's happened to Kip?'

Feeling really unhappy now, she went and found her mobile and called the vet's number. Her heart was beating fast. But the vet's phone was on voice mail.

'It's Laura Barton here,' she said. 'You've got my dog, Kip. How is he? I was worried because you didn't come this morning. Can you phone me when you get this message?' She left her mobile number.

Feeling lonely, sad and worried about Kip, Laura got a book and went to sit outside in the sunshine. But she couldn't think about the story. And after about ten minutes the sky went dark and it began to rain. The rain was very heavy, as if the sky had opened.

'Am I going to spend the afternoon in this cold barn on my own?' she wondered. 'Surely Nick will come back, now it's raining?'

* * *

Nick had been water-skiing for about an hour, but the weather had got so bad he could no longer see through the rain.

'I think we'd better give up,' his friend shouted, turning off the boat's engine and helping Nick climb onto the boat. They went back to the beach.

Nick was pulling off his wetsuit when he noticed the Land Rover arriving. It stopped beside his car and a man jumped out. Nick recognised the tall man who had been in the pub on their first evening. He had Kip with him.

'Do you know where this dog's owner is?' the man asked.

'Laura? Hi, I'm her boyfriend,' said Nick, holding out his hand to shake the other man's. 'How do you do? I'm Nick.'

'Here's your dog,' said the vet. 'Perhaps you'd like him back now?'

Nick laughed. 'It's not my dog! It's Laura's.'

'Ah. Well, where is she? I need to give him back to her,' said the vet.

'She's up at the barn, as far as I know,' said Nick. 'Could you take the dog up to her? I've got to get changed and pack up my things.'

Robert decided not to argue. He didn't like the way this man spoke to him, but he wasn't surprised. He'd met people like Nick before. People who came from London and behaved as if they were more important than everyone else.

Robert turned his Land Rover round and set off

for the barn again. He had more work to do this afternoon, and he needed to give this dog back. Once he'd returned Kip, he wouldn't have to have anything more to do with these two awful people.

He looked at Kip. He was a nice little dog, and Robert was sorry in a way to be giving him back.

'I'm sorry you have to live with owners like that,' he said to Kip, as he drove towards the barn. 'They clearly don't know how to look after you properly.'

* * *

Laura was in the barn cooking the blackberries. It was quite nice with the rain coming down. She tried to stop worrying about Kip. Then she heard the sound of a car engine again.

She looked out of the window through the rain. It wasn't the sports car this time. It was a Land Rover – it must be the vet at last. She went to the door.

The vet stood there in a long raincoat, holding Kip. He handed Laura the dog.

Laura took Kip in her arms, feeling a new love for the little dog now she had nearly lost him.

'Is he all right?' asked Laura. 'I've been so worried.'

'He's fine...now,' said the vet. 'I hope you've

checked the barn for more poison?'

'Yes, I have,' said Laura, feeling like a small schoolchild.

'I'm a busy man,' said the vet. 'I don't need unnecessary emergencies.'

'No, I understand that,' replied Laura.

'He's a country dog,' the vet said then. 'You shouldn't leave him alone in a flat all day.'

Laura looked at the vet. Why did he sound so annoyed with her? He knew nothing about her.

'I know that,' she said. She looked at him again, but she suddenly felt she couldn't speak any more, even though there was so much to say.

She wanted to tell him that Kip belonged to an old man who loved him. An old man who was at home all day. She wanted to say so much, but she couldn't. She didn't know why.

'How much do I owe you?' she asked instead.

'That'll be a hundred pounds, please,' the vet replied.

Her heart began to jump again. She didn't have a hundred pounds! Or at least she didn't have a hundred pounds to spend on the dog.

'Do I...do I have to pay now?' she asked, feeling

more stupid than ever.

The vet looked at her and for a moment Laura felt afraid that he was really angry. Then he surprised her, as he had done the night before.

'It's OK,' he said. 'Perhaps you could bring the money over to the surgery when you're passing.' He turned to leave. He'd noticed the lovely smell of blackberries cooking, coming from the kitchen, and it brought up memories for him he didn't want to think about.

'I'll bring the money to you tomorrow,' Laura said. 'I'm sorry...for the trouble.'

Laura felt again that she wanted to say more. She wanted to have a chance to explain herself. But at that moment Nick arrived in the sports car.

'What's going on?' he asked.

'I'm just arranging to pay the vet's bill,' said Laura. 'He's saved Kip's life!'

'How much money does he want?' asked Nick, as if the vet wasn't there.

'It's a hundred pounds,' said Laura. 'But it's OK. I'm going to pay him tomorrow after I've been into town.'

'A hundred pounds! Is that dog worth that much?' asked Nick.

The vet looked at Nick angrily. 'You wouldn't *be* spending a lot of money on him if you'd checked the barn for rat poison to begin with,' he said.

'We didn't expect there to *be* rat poison. What kind of a place uses rat poison?' asked Nick.

'Places where people don't want rats,' said the vet.

'But it's so old-fashioned! It's like going back a century round here!' said Nick and he laughed. The vet didn't even smile.

'Look,' said Laura. 'We made a mistake. You're right. We'll be careful in future. I'm going into town tomorrow. I'll get the money then. And,' she added, knowing it was always best to be polite in this kind of situation, 'thanks for saving Kip's life. I don't know what I'd have told Joseph if you hadn't.'

As the vet turned to leave he looked at Laura. He wondered who Joseph was. But he'd had enough of these two, so he drove away without asking.

Chapter 8
A terrible accident

Laura and Nick sat in the pub, eating supper.

'That's a nice little dog you've got there,' a voice said.

Laura looked up. The woman who was speaking to her was small and dark with shining blue eyes.

'Oh,' the woman said then, 'wasn't he at the vet's this morning?'

'Yes,' said Laura. 'How did you know?'

'Oh, I work there,' she said. 'I'm Maggie. I'm the vet's receptionist. I love animals. I've always loved them. Oh, look at him!'

'Ah,' said Nick. 'Then perhaps you can tell us why your vet's so rude?'

'Oh, he's not rude,' said Maggie. 'He's just sad. And if you knew what happened two years ago you'd understand why. He's hardly spoken to anyone since. Especially you city people. He's got no time for you.'

'Why's that?' Laura asked. She felt hurt, she realised, that Robert hadn't given her a chance just because she came from London.

'Well…' began Maggie. 'Do you mind?' she added, pulling up a chair.

'It's like this. Robert was going to be married to Chiara. She was Italian. She was a lovely girl – beautiful, kind *and* clever. She was training to be a doctor. Imagine! A vet and a doctor! So one evening she decides to go for a swim in the lake. It's a beautiful evening in early summer and it's still light. She and Robert quite often went swimming after work. But on this evening, Robert's working late, so he tells her he'll see her at the lake a bit later and she goes ahead on her own. There are some boys up from London, and they're messing about near the lake, talking about jet-skiing. There are quite a few people around, walking by the water, enjoying the evening.

'Chiara goes into the water and swims out. They say she swam along the golden path the sun made on the water as it went down. As I said, it was a beautiful evening.'

Maggie stopped and looked dreamily up at the ceiling for a minute. Then she went on.

'While she's out there, enjoying the sunset, the boys on the lake-side decide to go out on their jet-skis. The sun's quite low by now and possibly it's shining in their eyes...'

Maggie stopped and had some of her drink. She was enjoying telling this story, it was clear, and Laura and Nick were a good audience.

'...or perhaps they're drunk because, somehow, they don't see Chiara. They're going really fast and shouting and making a lot of noise. Suddenly... Bam! They hit her.'

Laura covered her ears. She didn't want to hear any more of this story. But Maggie wouldn't stop.

'They say she flew right up into the air. People say that for a few seconds she looked like a big bird, taking off from the water, but when she came back down, she was dead.'

Maggie looked up at Laura and Nick. Laura looked terrible. There were tears in her eyes. Nick looked annoyed.

'There's blood all over the water. And the boys on their jet-skis, they just disappear. The next day they've gone. Back to London. And nobody ever catches them.'

There was a few seconds' silence.

'That's terrible,' said Laura.

'Yes, and even more terrible, Robert arrived at the

lake just in time to see Chiara die. He saw it all. He heard the sound of the jet-ski hitting her body, and saw her fly up into the air.'

'Robert has had nothing to do with city people since then. And he's been trying to stop jet-skis on the lakes. He says they're not just dangerous, they're bad for the countryside and the wildlife. And some say he'll never get over Chiara's death and he'll live the rest of his life on his own. But that's only if I don't get my way!' she said laughing. 'He's really good-looking, don't you think so?' She looked at Laura as she said this and Laura felt herself go red.

* * *

It was Saturday morning. Laura made coffee on the tiny camping stove and took it up to Nick.

'Thanks, honey,' Nick said, taking the cup from her.

'Nick,' said Laura. She'd decided she needed to talk to him. She needed to know if she was going to spend any time with him at all this weekend.

'What are we going to do today? I thought perhaps we could go for a walk together. I don't feel I've seen you much since we got here. And there's a lovely hill we could walk up right behind the barn. There must be wonderful views from the top.'

'I tell you what,' said Nick. 'Why don't you come with me today? I could teach you how to jet-ski.'

Laura looked at him. His eyes were shining like the first time she'd seen him. It had been easy to like him then, when he first looked at her like this. Now, for some reason she didn't understand, it had no effect on her.

'I'm not sure,' she said. 'I don't think I'd be very happy jet-skiing after what that woman told us in the pub last night.'

'Oh, you don't want to worry about stories like that,' said Nick. 'These locals get very angry about tourists. They forget that actually we bring in a lot of money.'

'But don't you think she's got a good argument?' asked Laura.

'A good argument about what?' replied Nick.

'About stopping jet-skiing?' continued Laura.

'She wasn't suggesting stopping jet-skiing,' said Nick.

'OK, she wasn't suggesting it herself. She was telling us what the vet thinks,' said Laura.

'Was she? I thought she was just telling us that

he can't get over his girlfriend's death. He needs to accept it and move on. He can't expect everyone to give up their sports just because of one accident,' said Nick.

'But the point was that his girlfriend was killed by jet-skiers. Don't you think that's terrible?' asked Laura.

'Laura, I can jet-ski if I choose to. If that man's got a problem with it, he should either live somewhere else or shut up about it,' said Nick. He got out of bed.

'I'd *like* you to come with me,' he said. 'You should be pleased. I don't usually invite my girlfriends jet-skiing with me.'

'I'm sorry, Nick. I can't. Not after hearing that story. And anyway I've got Kip to think about.'

'Kip! All you ever think about is that dog. Well, if you're not coming,' Nick said, 'I want to get out on the lake right now. We've only got two more days.'

Laura gave up. 'OK. Look, Nick, if you're going out all morning again, please can I have the car? I'm going to take Kip for a walk, but after that I need to go into town to get some money. Then I need to pay the vet.'

'Sure. Drop me off and you can have the car for as

long as you like,' replied Nick.

Half an hour later Laura watched as Nick went noisily out across the lake, his jet-ski tearing into the peace of the morning. She thought of the story Maggie had told them last night. It was terrible!

'How could Nick go straight out there after such a story?' she wondered as she drove away from him. 'And I just can't understand why he wants to race over the lakes like that. For me the beauty of the Lake District is its peace. Why can't Nick understand that?'

Chapter 9

Alone again

Laura drove the car back up to the barn and found Kip. 'Let's walk,' she said. 'I need some air and exercise.'

She started walking up the hill behind the barn. It was a beautiful morning, the air washed clear by yesterday's rain. Soon they were high up, looking down on the countryside below. It was a wonderful view.

'Come on, Kip!' shouted Laura. 'Let's go right up to the top!' They climbed higher and higher until the lake looked tiny below them, and the jet-skis on it looked like flies.

When they got to the top, Laura found a rock to sit on. She took in big breaths of the sweet fresh air, and Kip sat beside her.

'This is so good for me!' Laura said to Kip. 'I really need space sometimes. It clears my mind. I wonder if I could live somewhere like this again.'

'I love these mountains and the fields and the woods. I think my dream would be to run my café in a small town, and live somewhere beautiful like this.

London is exciting, but it's so busy and noisy. I don't know if it's for me. And,' she said, looking down at Kip, 'if I lived somewhere like this, I could perhaps even get a little dog like you.'

She only began to think it was odd later, as she made her way back down the hill, that she hadn't included Nick in this dream life.

As she got to the road at the bottom of the hill, she saw a Land Rover coming towards her. Kip was running along ahead of her.

Laura's heart jumped. It was the vet! Was he going to tell her she shouldn't be walking on this side of the road? Tell her off for letting Kip run in the fields? Ask for the money from her again? Laura wished she could hide somewhere, but it was too late. The Land Rover came right up beside her and stopped, and Robert looked out of the window.

'How is he?' he asked, looking at Kip.

'He's fine. Much better,' said Laura. 'I'm bringing the money later today,' she said, before he could mention it. 'I'm going into town to do a bit of shopping. I'll get some money while I'm there.'

'Oh, OK,' said Robert.

There was a silence, so Laura began to talk. She

felt nervous.

'I want to look at some of the local food shops. I thought perhaps they could help. I'm looking for a supplier from this area. I'd like to sell some food from round here in my shop.'

'Your shop?' he asked.

'It's a food shop with a café,' she found herself explaining. 'An organic food shop.'

'Oh,' he said again. He was looking at her with surprise. 'Actually, there's a very good organic food shop in Cockermouth. My aunt runs it. She gets her cheeses from the farms round here.'

'Really? That sounds great,' said Laura.

'And I can easily give you the names and addresses of some cheese suppliers when you bring the money later,' he said.

'Thanks!' said Laura and smiled at him. But he was already driving away.

* * *

Back at the surgery that afternoon, Robert jumped out of his Land Rover.

Maggie was waiting at the door. It had begun to rain and she was standing under an umbrella. Robert leant across her and opened the door with his key. Maggie looked up at him, hoping he might return her look, but as usual Robert didn't seem to notice her.

'What have we got this afternoon?' he asked, as she started up the computer.

She read off the list of people who had booked in their animals. There was a sheep he needed to visit, and a pony, later on when he did his rounds. But right now there was a woman arriving with a rabbit that wasn't eating, and another one with a big dog.

'Oh,' said Maggie. 'And I forgot to tell you, that woman – the one with the lovely little dog called Kip – she phoned yesterday morning and left a message. She wondered why you hadn't brought the dog back. She sounded worried.'

Robert looked at Maggie. 'Why didn't you tell me yesterday?' he said.

'I didn't think it mattered,' she replied. 'I knew you'd gone that way anyway.'

Robert said nothing and disappeared into his surgery.

Later that afternoon he was just saying goodbye to a girl with a cat when Maggie put her head round the door of his surgery. She handed Robert a cup of tea.

'That lady called Laura is here,' Maggie said. 'She's got that nice little dog with her. She's paid, but she says you've got something for her. A farmer's address or something.'

Robert put his tea down. 'Yes, I know what she wants,' he said to Maggie. 'Send her in.'

Laura came into the room. She was holding Kip under one arm and for a second Robert felt his heart quicken, a feeling he'd almost forgotten. It was to do with the little dog, he thought. Perhaps it was simply that he wished he was holding it instead of Laura.

'So he's OK now? No more problems?' asked Robert, resting his hand on Kip's head. His hand touched Laura's arm by mistake and she quickly moved away.

'He's fine. Thanks,' said Laura, surprised that the vet was asking her again. He'd already asked her if Kip was OK this morning.

She looked at the vet. He was looking at Kip very lovingly, Laura thought. Then she thought, 'No, that's crazy. The vet sees dogs all the time. Why would he like Kip any better than any of the other dogs he cares for?'

Maggie interrupted them. 'Mrs Pierce wants to see you with her Labrador,' she said to Robert. 'He's behaving badly, and she wants him to see a psychologist.'

'OK. Tell her I'll be with her in just one moment,'

said Robert, and Maggie left the room.

Laura tried not to smile at the thought of a dog psychologist and she wondered if Robert was trying not to smile too.

He looked at Laura, and for a second their eyes met, before he looked away again.

'It sounds funny,' he said, as he copied an address onto a piece of paper. 'But I've got this idea that people often come to see me with their animals, not because the animal is sick, but because they need some help themselves.'

'Really? That's interesting,' said Laura, surprised that the vet was suddenly talking to her like this.

'Yes. This dog that behaves badly... It's actually the owner who is ill. She suffers badly from depression. She's the one who needs a psychologist, not the dog. Or perhaps,' he added, 'the dog needs a psychologist *because* the owner needs one.'

It was the longest sentence she'd ever heard him speak and Laura was surprised – surprised and interested in what he'd said.

'So do you tell the owners to go to a doctor? When you see that they're sick, I mean,' she asked him.

'That's not my job,' said Robert. 'I can listen, but it's not my job to tell them what to do.'

'I sometimes feel a bit like that in my café,' said Laura. 'People tell me all sorts of things, but I can't tell them what to do about it. Sometimes people just need to talk.'

'Exactly,' said Robert. 'Now, here are those addresses you wanted.'

'Thanks,' said Laura. 'I must go, and let you get on.'

Laura felt strange as she left the surgery. The vet had spoken more than he ever had before. And he'd spoken to her as if he knew she would understand what he was saying.

'I won't see him ever again now I've paid him,' she thought.

As she drove away she realised that this last thought made her feel sad.

'It's because I want to show him I'm not the hopeless Londoner he thinks I am,' she thought, trying to explain her feelings.

Chapter 10
A birth

Laura looked at the addresses on the paper the vet had given her. She took out a map. There was a farm that made and sold cheese quite near the barn. Yes, she could drive back to the barn and then walk to the farm with Kip.

Half an hour later Laura was walking towards the farm with Kip beside her. The farm was almost on the top of a hill. It was a hard walk across fields and up the hill, and the sky had clouded over again. It was going to rain.

Laura took Kip under one arm, and went to the farmhouse door and knocked. Some hens were running about in the farmyard.

Nobody came to the door. A cow was making a loud noise on the other side of the farmyard. It sounded as if it was in pain. Kip barked.

Laura knocked on the door again, then gave up and went across the farmyard towards the sound of the cow. Walking around a barn she saw a young man bent over a cow that was lying on its side. The man looked at her.

'She's having a baby,' he shouted, 'but the calf's got stuck. I've phoned the vet. I thought you were him.'

Laura didn't know what to do. 'I'm in the way,' she said. 'I wanted to ask about your cheese, but I'll come back another time.'

'You could help, actually,' said the man. 'Just until the vet arrives. If you could tie the dog up and hold the cow's head still.'

'Oh dear,' thought Laura. 'This is the last thing I expected.' She tied Kip's lead to a gate and went back to the farmer.

'Hold her head still and talk to her,' said the farmer. 'I'm going to have to tie a rope to the calf's leg. It's breech.'

Laura knew that breech meant the calf was coming out the wrong way round.

'It could be dangerous to the calf *and* its mother,' said the farmer.

The cow mooed loudly and painfully. Laura touched its nose gently. 'It's OK,' she said. 'It's going to be OK.'

'I'm going to need some help this end,' shouted

the farmer. 'We need to get this calf out quickly.'

Laura began to feel frightened. She had never done anything like this before. She went round to the cow's tail end and helped the farmer pull on the rope.

'It's coming,' he said.

The cow let out a loud cry again and the farmer pulled. His face was wet with sweat. The cow mooed loudly again.

'No, it's stuck. We'll have to give up in a minute. I just hope the vet gets here soon.'

At the mention of the vet again, Laura's heart jumped. Or was it just the effort of helping the calf out?

'Let's have one more try,' said the farmer, and Laura pulled as hard as she could.

After several more minutes, at last the calf was born. The farmer held it until it let out a cry, then put it on the ground. It shook itself. The cow turned and touched it and within a few minutes the calf stood up on thin legs.

Laura looked at it. 'Amazing!' she said. 'There's something so amazing about seeing an animal being born.'

'Yes. Thank goodness!' the farmer said. 'I thought

we'd lost them both. We were just in time.'

He turned to her. 'You weren't expecting this, were you? You came to ask about...What was it?'

'About cheese. I was...I was hoping you might let me taste your cheeses. I've got a shop in London and I'm looking for new suppliers. But perhaps this isn't a good time to ask.' Laura had untied Kip and was holding him again.

'No, it's fine. Cheese... Hmm. You'd better come into the house. If you don't mind waiting while I wash.'

Laura sat in the farmhouse kitchen and, when he'd washed, the farmer offered her some of his cheeses to taste.

'These are delicious. Really special,' said Laura. 'I'd definitely like to order some.'

'That's great!' said the farmer and he got out some paper to write down his email address.

'Oh goodness. Look at the time,' Laura said suddenly. 'I need to get Nick from the lake.'

'Nick?' asked the farmer.

'Yes. He's my boyfriend. He's jet-skiing,' Laura explained. 'I promised I'd be there by six so we could get to the pub early for a meal.'

She arranged to email the farmer when she got back to London, and set off across the fields with Kip running along beside her. She felt pleased with herself. The afternoon had turned out to be quite exciting, and she'd found some delicious cheese to sell.

Just as she disappeared into the trees, Robert's Land Rover pulled up at the farm.

'You're too late,' said the farmer, coming out of the house. 'The calf is born. And I think it's OK.'

'I'll check it over anyway,' said Robert. He knew this farmer well and each of his cows was special to him.

'I'm sorry it took me so long. There was another emergency at Top Farm. A horse with a broken leg.'

'Don't worry – I was lucky. A woman arrived just in time,' said the farmer. 'She helped me.'

'Oh?' said Robert.

'Yes. She'd come asking for cheese, for a shop she runs in London, but she ended up helping me instead. Quite an adventure for her.'

'Oh, that's good,' said Robert, realising that the farmer must be talking about Laura. 'So where is she now?'

'She had to go. To get her boyfriend from the lake so they could get to the White Bull early. Tourists obviously.'

'Yes,' said Robert. 'I think I've met them.'

'The worst sort,' said the farmer. 'Jet-skiers.'

'Well, *he* is. She doesn't seem to be interested,' said Robert. The farmer pulled a face, and Robert said no more.

After he'd checked the cow and calf, Robert drove back to the surgery, where Maggie was just clearing up.

'Thank goodness it's Saturday night, and I'm not on call,' he said.

Maggie, seeing that he was smiling, said, 'How about coming for a drink at the White Bull tonight?'

'Oh, OK,' Robert replied. And Maggie looked at him. She couldn't believe her luck.

'Did you just say yes?' she asked.

'Yes, I just said yes,' said Robert, and Maggie laughed and laughed.

Chapter 11

Two couples

Laura drove back to the lake and sat in the car. Nick was still out on the water and it had begun to rain hard. Kip sat beside her. They watched the rain come down, and the jet-skis out on the lake jumping across the water.

At last Nick came over. He threw his wetsuit into the car.

'Let's get straight to the pub. I'm ready to eat,' he said.

She was getting used to Nick's ways. He wasn't going to ask her what she would prefer to do. He made all the decisions and expected her to agree with them. They sat in silence as they drove.

After a few minutes, Laura felt uncomfortable with the silence.

'So, you had a good day?' she asked him.

'Great! You?' he answered.

'Yes. I went to find a cheese supplier for my shop, and ended up helping a cow give birth!'

'Good,' said Nick.

'Good?' Laura began to feel angry. Wasn't Nick even listening to her properly?

'No, Nick, it wasn't just good – it was amazing! Watching – *helping* a new life to begin. There's nothing like it. It made me think my life's quite dull.'

'What? Duller than a cow's?' Nick laughed.

'No, I mean duller than a vet's,' Laura replied.

'A vet's?' asked Nick.

'Yes. I mean that's a vet's job – helping animals to give birth. It's so important, so interesting and so moving,' said Laura.

'Was the vet there too?' asked Nick.

'No, it was just the farmer and me,' said Laura.

'Then the vet isn't doing a very good job, is he? He wasn't even there when he was needed. Now,' Nick said, taking her hand and smiling at her, 'what are we going to eat tonight?'

* * *

The pub was busier this evening.

'What are you going to have?' Nick asked Laura.

She looked at the menu for some time. She was finding it hard to decide. There were other thoughts going through her mind, making her feel unhappy and confused.

At last she said, 'I'll have the meat and vegetable pie. How about you?'

'Fish and chips,' he said. 'I've had enough of all this local food.'

'I'll order the food,' said Laura. 'And I'll get some drinks at the same time,' and she went to the bar.

* * *

Maggie and Robert were sitting on stools at the bar.

'Wasn't that Persian cat beautiful that came in this afternoon?' Maggie asked. 'It had the most amazing eyes!'

Robert smiled, but said nothing. Maggie was very sweet. But why did she only ever want to talk about animals – and usually the ones he was least interested in?

'You could do worse than get yourself a cat, you know,' Maggie went on. 'They're nice to have around and they take care of themselves.'

'Look, Maggie, I know you mean well, but I'm really not interested in getting a cat at the moment,' Robert said.

Maggie pulled a face, pretending to be hurt. 'Sorry,' she said. 'It's just, you know, I worry about you living all on your own.'

'Don't worry,' said Robert. 'It may be hard for

you to understand, Maggie, but there are people who like living alone better than sharing their house with anyone – anyone with two legs or anyone with four.'

'But you're a vet!' said Maggie.

'It doesn't mean I want to *live* with cats. Animals have a place, yes,' explained Robert. 'I like helping them out, as you know. I especially like to help farmers, and I felt really bad this afternoon that I missed helping that calf being born.'

'Ugh!' said Maggie, making a face.

'What do you mean "Ugh"?' asked Robert.

'I don't know – the thought of, you know, pulling a calf out of a cow,' said Maggie.

'Helping animals to give birth is actually the best part of my job,' Robert said. 'It's more exciting than giving cats medicine for their colds. And seeing an animal being born is beautiful.'

'What's so beautiful?' An older woman had come across the bar to talk to them. She had white-grey hair and was smartly dressed in a silk jacket and skirt.

'Barbara!' said Robert, standing up and kissing her. 'How nice to see you. What are you doing here?'

'I'm having dinner,' she said, nodding towards a man at a table on the other side of the bar. 'Ian invited me.'

'That's great!' said Robert. 'Maggie, this is my aunt, Barbara. She runs a food shop in Cockermouth. Barbara, this is my receptionist, Maggie.'

'How do you do, Maggie?' said Barbara.

She looked at Robert and his receptionist. 'So,' she thought. 'At last. Robert is beginning to be sociable again. And it looks as if he's got himself a girlfriend.'

'We've had a busy day,' Robert began to explain. 'Maggie suggested a drink and...' He stopped. He could feel something warm against his leg. He looked down and two brown eyes were looking up into his.

'Kip!' he said brightly.

'I'm so sorry.' Laura was hurrying towards them. 'He saw you and he just ran towards you,' Laura said to Robert. 'I couldn't stop him. He's clearly become very attached to you.'

Robert smiled at the dog, and then looked up at Laura.

'It's OK,' he said. 'Listen, it's good that you're here. This is my aunt Barbara. She runs the shop in Cockermouth I told you about this morning. Barbara, this is Laura.'

'Oh!' said Laura. 'How nice to meet you. I run a food shop too, but in London.'

Barbara looked at Laura, then at Robert.

'So...how do you know each other?' she asked. She knew Robert didn't like Londoners, and it seemed strange that he was being friendly to Laura.

'Oh, Robert saved Kip's life,' said Laura, pointing at her little dog.

'And you helped a cow give birth this afternoon,' Robert said suddenly. Laura looked at him.

'Yes,' she said. 'I...I just happened to be there... and, well, you weren't...'

'You're taking my work away from me,' said Robert without smiling.

Laura looked at him and felt afraid again. Was he really angry with her?

Then he smiled. 'Don't look so worried,' he said. 'I was joking.'

'No, but he's right!' said Maggie, looking straight at Laura. 'It can be dangerous trying to help with animals when you know nothing about them. The calf could have died.'

'Oh!' said Laura. 'But it didn't. And anyway I didn't mean to help. The farmer asked me to. There was nobody else there. He was waiting for...waiting for...'

'He was waiting for me,' Robert said to Maggie. 'But I was with that horse, the one with the broken leg.'

'Well, I must get back to Ian now. If you'd like to

visit my shop, I'd love to talk to you more,' Barbara said to Laura. 'I'll be in tomorrow morning, but I close at twelve. We always go for a good long walk on Sunday afternoons.'

'OK, I'd love to come,' said Laura. 'Thank you. It was very nice to meet you.'

As she walked back to Nick, Laura could feel Maggie's eyes watching her go.

Chapter 12
A new friend

Laura went back to Nick, while Kip stayed under Robert's feet. She tried not to think about Robert and Maggie sitting so comfortably together there, or the way Maggie had looked at her. She felt something, but didn't try to decide what it was. The good thing was that she was getting some new suppliers for her shop, and now she was going to visit that nice lady Barbara tomorrow. They could give each other ideas.

'Wow!' said Nick, as Laura sat down. 'Isn't that the woman we were talking to last night?'

'Yes,' said Laura. 'Why?'

'Well, she's lovely. I can't think why she's with that horrible vet.'

Laura looked back at the couple at the bar. She hadn't really looked at Maggie properly before.

'I suppose she is very pretty,' said Laura. 'But the vet is good-looking too, and he's quite nice really. They make a good couple.'

She was staring across the bar at the two people. Their heads were bent together as they chatted, and she wondered what they were talking about.

* * *

When Laura woke up the next morning, Nick had already gone out. There was a note in the kitchen. 'Out on the lake. Back at lunchtime,' it said.

Laura felt unhappy, but there was nothing she could do about it. She sat and looked at Kip.

'What's happening, Kip?' she asked the dog. 'Nick isn't the person I thought he was. And my guess is, I'm not the person he thought I was either. It's always the same! How do I do it? How do I always choose the wrong men?'

She thought again about their first night here. How she'd had to drive alone through the night to find the vet. It seemed that when Nick didn't want to do something he just didn't do it. And his ideas about the countryside here made her unhappy too, however much she tried to understand them.

'He doesn't really want me here,' she thought. 'I'm beginning to think he's just not right for me.'

Suddenly Laura remembered that Barbara had invited her to see her shop this morning, and she suddenly felt brighter.

'I've got my own life to live,' she thought. 'Who

needs men anyway, eh Kip?'

She looked at her watch. It was quarter past ten now. It was probably half an hour's drive to Cockermouth. If she left now she would get there in plenty of time.

Luckily, Nick had left the car for her and she got in and set off to Cockermouth.

It was a beautiful morning. Yesterday's rain had made everything shine like glass in the morning sunshine and the colours were bright. She felt clear-headed now she had thought carefully about her relationship with Nick.

'I'm going to work hard at my business,' she thought, 'and learn what I can from Barbara. I'm not going to worry about relationships for now.'

Barbara's shop was at one end of the High Street. Laura parked the car and walked along the street with Kip. It was an interesting little town with some nice shops.

Laura found Barbara's shop and went in.

Barbara came out from the back of the shop, smiling warmly.

'Hello, my dear. How nice of you to come,' she said.

'Janie's looking after the shop for me, so we can talk. Come through to the back.'

Laura followed her, noticing the jars of interesting foods on sale.

'So,' Barbara said, several minutes later, 'tell me about your shop, how you started, what you sell and so on.'

The shop was at the front of a large house, and they were now sitting in the kitchen. Barbara gave Laura a glass of home-made lemonade.

Laura told Barbara all about her shop in London and they talked for ages, not noticing the time.

'You must taste these pies,' Barbara said, getting something out of the oven. 'A local woman makes them for me. They would go down well in your café. Robert loves this one.' She handed Laura a piece of delicious-looking pie.

'Robert?' asked Laura, biting into the pie.

'Yes. He loves my food,' said Barbara. 'What do you think of him? He can seem a bit unfriendly, but he's got a good heart. Do you know why he's so quiet?'

'I heard the terrible story about his girlfriend,' said Laura.

'Yes. It was an awful thing,' Barbara said. 'It's affected him very deeply.'

'Yes,' said Laura.

'It wasn't just her death,' said Barbara, 'it was the fact that nobody ever caught the people who killed her. Robert feels that while people are still allowed to use jet-skis on the lakes, another accident may happen.'

'Well, he's got a point,' said Laura.

'But he needs to move on,' said Barbara. 'It's not good to hold on to such a terrible memory. He needs to forget what happened and start to live a full life again.'

'It must be very hard for him,' said Laura, remembering the terrible description Maggie had given them in the pub. 'Anyway, isn't he seeing his receptionist these days?'

'Well, he was with her last night,' said Barbara. 'But she isn't his type, if you ask me. Anyway,' she went on, 'what do you think of the pies?'

'They're perfect!' said Laura, slowly taking in everything this woman was telling her. 'And you say Robert likes them too?'

'Oh, he likes all good food,' said Barbara. 'Or at

least he used to. Before Chiara died he used to be a very good cook himself. Then he lost interest in everything after she died. Everything except his work, that is. He really cares about the farmers and their animals. He's a good man, he really is.'

'Yes. And I'm very thankful to him. For two things: introducing me to you and for saving Kip's life.' Laura touched Kip's head.

'He's a nice little dog. You must be very attached to him,' said Barbara.

'Oh, he's not mine,' replied Laura. 'I'm looking after him for the old man who lives next door to me – he had to go into hospital the day before we came up to the Lakes. I don't really want a dog myself, not in London where they don't get much exercise. But it's funny how you get attached when you're with them all day.'

'Yes, I'm sure you do,' said Barbara. She leant back and smiled at Laura. 'So have you enjoyed your holiday in the Lakes?'

'Oh yes, I love it here,' said Laura with feeling. 'I've always loved it. I came here as a child. I thought perhaps it had changed, but it's just as beautiful.'

'It's busier than it used to be. The lakes get very

busy with people doing water sports.'

'Yes, that's changed. I came here with Nick, my boyfriend. He likes jet-skiing, but I'm not interested. I prefer walking. So Kip and I have been out walking by ourselves.'

'Oh, well, listen! Why don't you come with us this afternoon? I told you we go on a walk every Sunday after lunch. Would you like to join us? There are quite a few people coming and you'd be most welcome.'

'Oh, I'd love to,' said Laura.

'We're meeting at Coniston Lake at two o'clock. I'll look forward to seeing you later.'

Chapter 13
On the walk

'You went off without telling me where you were going!' Nick said crossly when Laura arrived back at the barn.

'I'm sorry, Nick. You went off without me, and I forgot to tell you I had to be in Cockermouth before twelve.'

'OK. Well, I want to get back on the water, so let's go!'

'We haven't had any lunch,' said Laura.

'I had a sandwich while I was waiting for you,' said Nick. 'Really, Laura, I don't want to waste any more time. We're leaving tomorrow.'

'Nick, all you seem to think about is your water sports! I have to say that I'm finding it rather difficult to accept.'

Nick stopped on his way to the car with an armful of wetsuits and looked back at Laura.

'Are you? You knew this was why I was coming to the Lakes. It's why I usually come alone. I asked you to come because I *thought* you were the kind of woman who would understand.'

'I do understand, up to a point. But Nick, we've hardly had any time together,' said Laura.

'That's because you aren't interested in jet-skiing,' Nick replied.

'No, I'm not...' Laura started.

'And because you brought that stupid dog with you!' Nick went on.

'Nick, that's not true,' Laura said.

'You spent the first night driving round the countryside looking for that bad-tempered vet,' Nick said.

'That was one night! And Nick, I had no choice, I was doing it for Joseph,' Laura said.

'Exactly. You were putting an old man before me,' said Nick.

'Nick, the dog nearly died! But since then we've had three days here and we've spent no time together. You're always out on the lake!' said Laura.

'Then why don't you come with me? Perhaps you would enjoy it,' said Nick.

'No, I wouldn't enjoy it. Because I care about what the local people here think, and you don't,' said Laura.

'No, Laura, I don't care! If you think I'm going to

stop doing the thing I enjoy most, you're wrong! I work 24/7 to earn enough money to live, and this is my big interest,' said Nick.

'It's just that I can't believe you don't care that a woman *died*,' said Laura.

'Yes, she died. It's not my fault she died. She was swimming in a lake while people were jet-skiing! That's why she died. If it was anyone's fault, it was her own!' said Nick.

'And jet-skis are so bad for the...' said Laura.

Nick had got into the car and was starting the engine angrily. Laura ran to the car.

'I'm sorry, Nick,' she said. 'I shouldn't say these things. I can't help it. I feel things so strongly sometimes and I can't just keep quiet about them.' Nick didn't answer. Laura got into the car next to him. 'Look Nick, if you're going jet-skiing again please can I have the car this afternoon? I've been invited on a walk and I'd really like to go.'

'A walk? Who with?' asked Nick.

'With a woman – the one I met in the pub last night. The one with the shop in Cockermouth.'

'Oh, OK. You can have the car,' said Nick, without looking at her.

* * *

That afternoon, Laura went back to meet Barbara and her friends. She was looking forward to walking with someone who knew the Lakes well.

As she drove she realised she felt sad. It wasn't working with Nick, and she already knew what would happen when they got back to London. Once they were back in their own lives it would be over. Laura thought of her flat and her job. Yes, they kept her busy. But how empty and pointless they seemed when there was nobody to share them with. It was so hard to find anyone who really understood what she was trying to achieve in her life.

She looked at Kip. 'No wonder some people just choose dogs for friends,' she said out loud. 'You're a lot less complicated.'

She arrived at the meeting place Barbara had told her about, and stood feeling a little shy. There were several older people there, wearing walking boots and carrying sticks. Suddenly Kip jumped to his feet and barked happily.

Laura looked up. Coming across the field from the village was Robert. Laura felt surprised. Robert arrived at the group and stood, silent, among them.

Barbara went over to Laura and whispered in her ear. 'I persuaded Robert to come,' she said. 'It's the first time he's agreed to a group walk for...well, for years. We should be pleased.'

They started walking along the bottom of the hills. Kip wanted to go to Robert and at last Laura let him take her to him.

'Hi,' she said.

'Barbara invited me for this walk,' he said, his head down, as if he was embarrassed. 'I don't usually enjoy being in a group – I prefer walking alone. But she wanted me to come and I gave in.'

They were walking along beside a stream, and the air smelt fresh and clean.

Soon they started to climb and the countryside fell away below them. Robert walked ahead, with Kip at his heels, so Laura began to walk beside Barbara. They chatted easily together about their shops.

'I've been hearing about Laura's shop and café,' Barbara told Robert later when they all stopped for a rest. 'It sounds lovely. We've already agreed my pies would sell very well there.'

'Good. That's excellent,' said Robert.

Kip came running over towards Robert again.

'That dog of hers seems to like you, Robert,' said Barbara. 'Well, it's not hers, of course, but...'

'What do you mean?' asked Robert.

'Oh, didn't she say? He belongs to an old man who had to go into hospital just before she came away. She's looking after it for him.'

'Oh!' said Robert, suddenly feeling everything fall into place. 'Oh, now I see.'

And he looked across the group at Laura. She was definitely different to what he had first thought. So the dog wasn't hers. She wasn't a terrible city type who kept a dog because it was fashionable, as he'd thought. 'Yet how can she go out with that awful man?' he wondered.

They continued to climb up the hill. Barbara turned round to wait for a friend, so Robert and Laura found themselves walking along side by side.

Robert nodded towards the woman Barbara was waiting for. 'She's called Mrs Fellows,' Robert said. 'She called me out one night because her cat was sneezing. The cat was fine, but *she* talked for half the night. Do you see what I mean?'

'You mean, she's the one who needed you, not the cat?'

'Yes,' answered Robert.

'Do you think everyone who brings an animal to see you has a problem of their own?' asked Laura.

'Not everyone, no,' Robert replied.

He looked sideways at her and Laura felt at last that he was warming to her.

'What about me?' Laura asked suddenly. 'That night I came to see you – did you think I needed help, not Kip?'

'Ah,' said Robert, smiling suddenly. 'Well, Kip did need help. Kip ate something that wasn't good for him. But perhaps you're doing something that isn't good for you! I think that could be true.'

'Like what?' asked Laura, laughing. She enjoyed this game. It reminded her of the one she played with Jo in the shop, guessing about people and what they did.

'Only you know that,' said Robert. Then he threw a stick for Kip and began to run after him, while Laura was left wondering, 'What does he mean?'

Chapter 14
Robert's house

Two hours later they arrived back at the bottom of the hills.

'That was a lovely walk,' said Laura to Barbara. 'Thank you so much for asking me along. I enjoyed it and so did Kip. I'd better get going now though. We're leaving tomorrow and I've got to pack.'

'Well, don't forget to phone or email me with your orders for the shop,' said Barbara. 'Or about anything else you may want. It's been a pleasure meeting you. Now then, Robert,' she said, turning to the vet, 'didn't you say you'd left the Land Rover at the garage and you needed a lift home?'

'I did,' said Robert.

'And Laura, you're staying over in Robert's direction, aren't you? You don't mind giving him a lift, do you?' asked Barbara.

Laura was afraid she was going to go red. She didn't know why.

'That's fine,' she said, letting her hair blow over her face.

'Thanks,' he said.

'And,' said Barbara, looking at Laura, 'I'll get the first order to you by mid-November.'

'If you don't mind, that would be great. In time for Christmas.' Laura looked into Barbara's eyes and felt as if she had made a friend. So why did she also feel that somehow this woman was tricking her?

Robert sat next to Laura in the sports car. He seemed too tall for the passenger seat in this tiny car.

'How strange this is,' thought Laura. 'How odd that he is suddenly here beside me, in Nick's car, when I thought...I thought... What did I think? I thought he hated me! I thought he had no time for city people!' Then she remembered what he had said up the mountain.

'What did you mean,' she asked, 'when you said perhaps I was doing something that wasn't good for me?'

'Ah,' said Robert. 'Only you know the answer to that.'

They were silent for a few minutes as Laura drove up a small road. Then Robert said, 'OK, my house is just up this road here. Thank you very much for the lift.'

‘That’s OK,’ Laura said as he got out.

He stood for a moment with his back to Laura, as if he was deciding what to do – to walk into his house or turn round.

Then he suddenly turned to her and said, ‘I don’t suppose you...you’d like a cup of tea?’

Laura looked at her watch. Nick would probably be out on the lake for another half an hour at least. She could take a few minutes to have a cup of tea with the vet. She felt pleased that he’d asked her. From what Maggie had said, he wasn’t usually very sociable. Perhaps now he and Maggie were becoming close, he was learning to relax with other people. Perhaps Maggie was helping him get over Chiara at last.

Kip was barking happily and looking at Robert with an open mouth as if he was smiling.

‘I think Kip’s decided for me!’ she said.

Robert’s house was large and old, though surprisingly warm and light. He led her into a big sitting room with French windows that looked out over a beautiful view of the hills.

He disappeared through a door into what must be the kitchen, and Kip followed him, looking very much at home.

'Hey, Kip, come here,' said Laura, following the little dog, but Kip was already lying down near Robert's feet.

'He remembers,' said Robert, and he smiled. Laura hadn't seen him smile much before. He had a wide mouth, and now it lit up his face as if the sun had just come out.

'You know, I want to thank you again for saving Kip's life,' Laura said shyly, looking up at Robert.

He was pouring milk into two mugs of tea. 'It's just my job,' he said.

'Yes, but I don't know what I'd have said to Joseph if he'd died. I felt terrible. I wasn't used to having a dog. I didn't think to check the barn.' She felt nervous of Robert even now, and when she was nervous she kept talking.

'And is Joseph a very good friend?' he asked.

'Yes. He's a dear old man who lives next door to me in London. He was taken ill the night before we came here. He asked me to look after Kip for him. He said he was frightened Kip might die before he did. I think he was frightened that if Kip died, he'd have no more reason to live. He's alone. He only has his dog.'

'Let's go and sit in there,' Robert said, and they went back through to the lovely sitting room. Outside, sheets of rain moved across the hills and trees.

'So, if Kip had died, the old man would have had no reason to live,' he repeated. 'I know that feeling...'

Laura waited, realising Robert was about to tell her about Chiara, about himself. She didn't want to speak, didn't want to break the silence that waited to be filled with his words.

He was standing at the window, looking out onto the countryside. She looked at his wide shoulders in his big hand-knitted jumper; his long legs in old corduroy trousers; his fair hair that looked as if it hadn't been brushed. And suddenly she knew for certain why he made her feel so nervous. It was because she found him so attractive.

She wished she didn't. She wished she'd never seen him. She wished she'd never come on this weekend to the Lakes. Because one thing was certain. There was no way this man would ever look at her in that way. He was with Maggie now. And although things were not going well with him, she was still with Nick.

'I've been completely wrong about you,' Robert

said suddenly, turning round and looking at her. 'I owe you an apology.'

'No, no, it's fine,' said Laura.

'I was rude and unpleasant to you. I thought it was you out on your jet-ski that morning. I thought it was your dog and that you didn't know how to care for him properly. I thought...I thought you just had a dog to be fashionable. But I was wrong. I hope you accept my apology,' he said.

'Of course I accept your apology,' said Laura.

'I mean...what I'm trying to say is that in fact you're the complete opposite to what I thought. You're thoughtful, and so very kind to look after this little dog for an old man on your weekend away. My problem is...my problem is I find it hard to...to... believe in anyone since my girlfriend died. I really felt I had no reason to live for a long time after she was killed.'

'That must be quite normal. Anyone would feel like that,' said Laura.

'Then my reason became stopping people jet-skiing. Apart from work, it was all I cared about,' Robert went on. 'I hated everyone that had anything to do with it. It's not good to hate people like that.'

'You couldn't help it. It's understandable. And it is awful to see jet-skis on these beautiful lakes. They look horrible and they sound terrible!' Laura said.

'I want to stop hating people all the time. I want to feel something good again. I'd like to feel...'

'What?' asked Laura quietly.

'Well, what I'm trying to say is, I think I'm beginning to feel something...for someone...again,' said Robert.

Laura suddenly felt breathless. She was afraid she was going to stop breathing altogether. She didn't want him to tell her about his feelings for Maggie. She simply didn't want to hear it. Not now she was beginning to have feelings for this man herself.

'I must go,' she said, standing up and putting her tea cup down. 'I need to get Nick from the water sports centre. Come on, Kip!'

Chapter 15 Two goodbyes

Laura wanted to get out of the room, out of the house, as quickly as possible. She wasn't sure where Robert was heading with his conversation, but she was afraid of it. She must go. She must go before she got in any deeper.

Robert followed her through to the front door.

'Well,' he said, 'I guess it's goodbye. Goodbye, Kip, and goodbye, Laura. When are you leaving?'

'Tomorrow,' she said. 'So goodbye. And thank you.'

He put his hand on the door. 'You're not angry? You understand what I've been trying to say?'

'Of course. We all make mistakes about people,' said Laura. 'When I first saw you in the pub, I thought you were a hill-walking poet,' she said.

He laughed. 'Well, I do enjoy hill-walking, so that part is true,' he said. 'And in fact I do write poems sometimes, so you weren't completely wrong.'

She smiled. 'I've got to go,' she said, but Robert's hand was still on the door and he hadn't opened it.

'Goodbye, Laura,' he said again, and she looked at

him. And for the first time she saw that his eyes were looking right into hers.

And then she knew it was happening. She knew

that there was nothing she could do to stop it. She was falling for this man. A man who was still in love with his dead girlfriend. A man who had just got together with another woman.

There were tears in her eyes as Laura drove away from Robert's house, back towards the lake.

'What has happened?' she wondered. 'How can this possibly have happened? I came here with Nick and I've fallen in love with someone else.'

She drove along angrily, and the rain fell heavily as she went.

'Normally I like someone, and then find out that I don't like them. This time I met someone who seemed to hate me, and I've found out that I like – no, I love him! Robert is so different to Nick. He's so kind! He's so thoughtful! We think like each other...'

The thoughts went round and round in her head as she drove.

'Nick isn't the person I thought he was after all, and I don't want to be with him. And Robert is someone I want to be with, but I can't! I must stop feeling anything right now.' She looked at Kip on the seat beside her. 'Help me, Kip,' she said. 'Help me to forget the vet!'

* * *

The next morning Laura and Nick got up early, ready to leave. Laura felt unhappy again. How could she sit next to Nick for another six hours in that tiny car all the way back to London? It was clear they had nothing more to say to each other. It was clear their relationship wasn't working.

'Hurry up!' said Nick. 'I don't want to get back too late. I've got a busy week.'

'OK,' said Laura. 'I'm ready. My bag's in the car. Come on, Kip!' she called. 'Time to go back to Joseph.'

Nick was just getting into the car when Laura's mobile rang. Laura answered it.

'Hello?'

'Laura Barton?' a woman asked.

'Yes,' replied Laura.

'This is Nurse Jones at St Thomas's Hospital. I believe you are a friend of Mr Joseph Donaldson?'

'Oh yes. How is he?' asked Laura.

'I'm sorry to tell you that Joseph died in the night,' the nurse said.

'What?' asked Laura quietly.

'I'm sorry. I know it's bad news, but he was very poorly and it was peaceful,' the nurse said.

Laura tried to speak, but all she could say was, 'But I have his dog.'

'Yes. Can you keep it? I'm sure Joseph would be happy for you to have it,' the nurse said.

'Oh, I'd never thought of keeping a dog. I have a small flat and...' Laura started. She could feel tears starting to run down her face.

'Anyway, I'm sorry to give you bad news,' the nurse said.

When the nurse had said goodbye, Laura sat in silence for a few moments.

'Who was that?' Nick asked.

'It was the hospital. Joseph died. They want me to keep the dog.'

'You're not keeping that dog!' said Nick. 'It's already cost you over a hundred pounds and been more trouble than it's worth.'

Laura looked at him. There were tears in her eyes.

'What's the matter?' Nick asked impatiently.

'Nick! My friend has just died. And all you can think about is how much the dog has cost me.'

'I'm sorry,' said Nick. 'I am, really. I wasn't thinking. It's just... What are you going to do with Kip in your tiny flat?'

'I don't know! I didn't expect this. I need to think for a moment.'

Laura walked up past the barn and stood looking at the view, touching Kip's head, thinking about Joseph. About the way he'd held her hand and said, 'You will take care of him, won't you?'

Kip had no idea his owner had died. It seemed so sad. 'What am I going to do with you?' she said to Kip.

Then it came to her like a bright light that made her want to jump up and run as fast as she could down the hill.

'Come on, Kip!' she said. 'We're going to see the vet again.'

Chapter 16
At the station

'Nick, would you mind driving me and Kip to the vet's surgery?' she asked gently.

'The vet? That vet again?' asked Nick.

'Yes, Nick, the vet again. I need to ask him if he'd like to have Kip. I've got a feeling they were meant for each other.'

'OK,' said Nick. 'You started this weekend at the vet's, so I guess it's right that you end it there too.'

'After that please could you take me to the station?' said Laura. 'I'll get the train home. I can't come back with you. You know that, don't you?'

'What are you saying, Laura? What's this about?' Nick asked.

'Look, Nick. It isn't working between us, is it? I need time to think.'

Nick looked at her. 'Is our relationship over?' he asked.

'What do you think?' Laura said.

'I should have guessed,' he said. 'This is why I don't usually bring women on holiday with me. It never works.'

'But isn't it better that we know?' said Laura. 'Isn't it better that we find out now, instead of in a year's time, that we have nothing in common?'

'I guess it is,' said Nick.

For a moment Laura felt sorry for him. It was as much of a disappointment to him as it was to her. But they both knew that she was right.

* * *

Robert looked down at Kip. 'So,' he said, 'I've got a friend at last.'

He felt near to tears. He didn't know why. He picked the dog up and it touched his cheek with its nose.

It was odd. He wasn't alone now, so why did he have a terrible feeling of emptiness, almost as bad as just after Chiara had died? It was so painful that he felt like hiding his face in Kip's fur and crying.

Then it hit him at last. It wasn't enough to have Kip. He wanted Laura too. He hated the thought that she had gone, that he would never see her again.

It was the first time he'd had feelings like this for...how long had it been? But Laura had Nick, and they were on their way back today. Back to the city and the lives they enjoyed down there, full of money and drinking and clothes and the other things people did in the city.

* * *

Laura sat alone on the station platform. Nick had left her at the station and gone back to London. She felt alone.

At least she knew that Kip had found a home, the best home possible. Joseph would have been pleased, she was certain of that.

When the train came into the station at last, she got on slowly, wishing that she didn't have to leave.

She sat in a corner of the train and went over the last couple of hours in her mind. Robert had taken Kip immediately. He hardly had to be asked.

'Of course I'll have him!' he'd said, a smile lighting up his face. Laura felt again like kissing him, as she had on the first night when he'd taken Kip home with him. But Maggie had been there, watching from the door, like a silent warning.

Laura sighed.

The train hurried south between fresh green hills that rose to either side. Soon she would be back in the city, back in her shop. This weekend, the beauty of the hills, Robert and Kip would just be memories.

* * *

The morning surgery was over and Robert had gone home for lunch. The house felt so empty. Robert looked at Kip, who looked back at him questioningly.

'What have I got to lose?' he asked the little dog.

He picked up his mobile. Sure enough, Laura's mobile number was on it, on the list of people who had phoned him recently.

'Laura,' he said when she answered. 'I know this is crazy. I know I sound mad. But I just wanted to speak to you again.' There were a few seconds of silence.

'Are you home yet?' he asked.

'No, I didn't drive back with Nick. I'm on a train. Nick and I are finished. I didn't want to go back with him.'

'A train? What...? What's the next station?' Robert asked.

'Oxenholme,' Laura replied.

'Oxenholme? Can you get off there? Get off and wait for me! I'll come and get you. We need to talk,' Robert said quickly. 'You know something's happening between us, don't you?'

'Robert, I can't. I've got to get back to London. Jo

is expecting me back in the shop tomorrow.'

'You can get a later train. Please,' said Robert.

Laura listened to his voice. How could she fight it?

'OK,' she said at last. 'I'll get off at Oxenholme.'

'Wait at the station,' said Robert. 'I'll be there as soon as I can.'

* * *

Laura sat on the station platform at Oxenholme feeling cold. 'What am I doing?' she wondered. 'Am I crazy? I need to be at work tomorrow. But I need to see Robert again. And he wants to see me! I can't possibly let him go.'

At last she looked up to see Robert and Kip coming towards her, and she knew after all she was doing the right thing.

Robert ran up to her on the platform and put his arms around her.

'The minute you left, I knew I couldn't just let you go,' he said. 'Will you come back with me, just for a few hours? You can get a later train.'

'But...but what will Maggie say?' she asked.

'Maggie? My receptionist? What do you mean, what will she say?' Robert asked.

'I thought you and she were...I thought... Aren't

you going out with her?'

Robert put his head back and laughed.

'I'm sorry,' he said. 'I can't think of a crazier idea! It's you I like. It's you I need. I haven't felt like this for years.'

Before she could argue Laura found herself next to Robert in the Land Rover, driving away from the station.

As Robert drove down the small road towards the lake, he tried not to think of that night two years ago. He put his hand on Kip's head as they came through the trees towards the lake. He held his breath as he waited for it to happen. The thing that always happened. The terrible sounds, the lights and screams.

They were beside the lake now. He waited. There was nothing.

He looked out across the water. Nothing. Just the light of the afternoon sun shining gently on the still water.

It was silent. It was beautiful. He felt odd, as if he was lighter than he'd been before. He felt as if his chest was full.

'What is this?' he thought. 'What's happening?'

And then he realised. He felt happy. For the first time in two years he felt happy.

He reached out his hand again and took Laura's hand, and then he looked at her and she smiled.

'You know when you offered to take Kip home with you after he ate the poison?' Laura said. 'I wanted to kiss you.'

'Why didn't you?' asked Robert.

'Because I thought you hated me,' she said.

He stopped the Land Rover then and moved towards her. 'You can kiss me now,' he said.

And the sun lit up their faces as they kissed.

After reading

读后活动

1. Write a newspaper report about Chiara's death.
2. Write a description of the Lake District.
3. Think of another title for *Love in the Lakes* and explain why it would be good.
4. Make a list of the different animal cases Robert worked on as a vet in the story.
5. Write a comparison of the characters of Nick and Robert.
6. Make a quiz about this story for other students, e.g. some true/false questions or some correct/incorrect sentences.
7. Write an email to the author, Penny Hancock, telling her what you liked and didn't like about the story.
8. What do you think will happen between Robert and Laura? Write some paragraphs explaining how their lives change after the end of the story.
9. Choose one of the minor characters in the story – e.g. Maggie or Barbara – and write some paragraphs about them, inventing more about their lives.

Learning guide | 学习指导

Chapter 1

New words 生词

- crash /kræʃ/ *n.* 撞车；碰撞声 *v.* 碰撞，撞击
- emergency /iˈmɜːdʒənsi/ *n.* 突发事件，紧急情况
- lamb /læm/ *n.* 羔羊，小羊
- organic /ɔːˈgænɪk/ *a.* 有机的
- sneeze /sniːz/ *v.* 打喷嚏
- surgery /ˈsɜːdʒəri/ *n.* 诊所，诊室
- vet /vet/ *n.* 兽医

Phrases & expressions 短语和表达

- in fear 惊恐地
- on call（尤指紧急情况下）随叫随到，待命
- prefer to do sth. 更喜欢做某事
- think of...as... 把……看作……

Cultural note 文化点滴

- the Lakes: 湖区 (Lake District)，英格兰西北部坎布里亚郡的一片乡村地区，是受欢迎的度假胜地，以湖泊与群山而闻名，并因 19 世纪初诗人华兹华斯以及其他湖畔诗人 (Lake Poets) 的作品而著称。

Reading exercises 阅读练习

1. Does Robert really see an accident and hear a scream as he is driving home? If so/not, where is the crash?
2. Why doesn't Robert eat at home very often? (Two reasons)
3. Why do you think his house is 'silent now'?
4. What do the local people think about Robert?
5. Why doesn't he sleep much at this time of year?

Chapter 2

New words 生词

- alarmed /əˈlɑːmd/ *a.* 惊恐的，受惊的
- arty /ˈɑːti/ *a.* 附庸风雅的，装作爱好艺术的
- bang /bæŋ/ *n.*（突然的）巨响 *v.* 猛敲，砸
- cappuccino /ˌkæpuˈtʃiːnəʊ/ *n.* 卡布奇诺（一种热牛奶咖啡）
- designer /dɪˈzaɪnə(r)/ *n.* 设计师
- flash /flæʃ/ *v.* 闪烁，闪光
- gown /gaʊn/ *n.* 长袍，长外衣
- slipper /ˈslɪpə(r)/ *n.* 拖鞋
- thankful /ˈθæŋkfl/ *a.* 感到庆幸的
- thriller /ˈθrɪlə(r)/ *n.* 惊悚电影或小说

Phrases & expressions 短语和表达

- ask sb. out 约某人出去
- bedside light 床头灯
- dressing gown 晨袍，晨衣
- heart attack 心脏病发作

- let sb. down 使某人失望
- pass the time 打发时间，消磨时光
- put on 打开（开关）
- sports car 跑车
- water sports 水上运动

Cultural notes 文化点滴

- Paul Smith: 保罗·史密斯，英国时尚品牌，其最受人追捧的是内里的些许叛逆精神——表面是绅士却偷着“耍坏”——这也是设计师 Paul Smith 的英式幽默。Paul Smith 的设计主要以朴实、简单为理念。另外，七彩条子也是 Paul Smith 的标志。
- Thames: 泰晤士河，英国最长的河流，也是最重要的水路，同时也是英国的母亲河。

Reading exercises 阅读练习

1. Who is Joseph and what happens to him?
2. What does Laura have to do while Joseph is in hospital?
3. Why might Kip be a problem for Laura at the weekend?
4. How did Laura meet Nick?
5. Which of these facts is true?
   a) Nick is a bank manager / a designer / a teacher.
   b) Nick rides a bike / a motorbike.
   c) Nick likes rock climbing / motor sports.
6. How does Laura feel about Nick?

Chapter 3

New words 生词

- blonde /blɒnd/ *a.*（头发）金黄色的
- guilty /ˈɡɪlti/ *a.* 内疚的
- intelligent /ɪnˈtelɪdʒənt/ *a.* 聪明的，理解力强的
- jet-skiing /ˈdʒetˌskiːɪŋ/ *n.* 水上摩托艇运动
- pheasant /ˈfeznt/ *n.* 野鸡
- playfully /ˈpleɪfəli/ *ad.* 开玩笑地
- redo /ˌriːˈduː/ *v.* 重做
- tut /tʌt/ *n.*（书面语中表示反对、厌烦或同情的）啧啧声
- wetsuit /ˈwetsuːt/ *n.* 潜水衣

Phrases & expressions 短语和表达

- by the light of... 借助……的光线
- keep an eye open for... 密切注意，留心
- make up one's mind 下定决心
- set off 出发，动身
- take hold of... 握住，抓住
- turn away from... 厌恶，对……感到厌烦

Cultural note 文化点滴

• Wordsworth: 华兹华斯（William Wordsworth，1770—1850），英国浪漫主义诗人，曾当上桂冠诗人。华兹华斯与柯勒律治（Samuel Taylor Coleridge）、骚塞（Robert Southey）同被称为“湖畔诗人”（Lake Poets）。

Reading exercises 阅读练习

1. Where are Nick and Laura going?
2. Read the extracts and answer the questions.
   a) 'He had a heart attack.' Who did?
   b) 'He never usually invited his girlfriends away with him.' Who didn't?
   c) 'He'll have to go in the back, on top of the luggage.' Who will?
   d) 'I can cook when we arrive.' Who can?
   e) 'He was interesting-looking...with an intelligent face.' Who was?
   f) 'They aren't very friendly around here.' Who aren't?

Chapter 4

New words 生词

- barn /bɑːn/ *n.* 谷仓
- fault /fɔːlt/ *n.* 过错，过失
- heartbroken /ˈhɑːtbrəʊkən/ *a.* 极度伤心的
- heating /ˈhiːtɪŋ/ *n.* 供暖系统和设备
- poison /ˈpɔɪzn/ *n.* 毒药
- properly /ˈprɒpəli/ *ad.* 适当地，正确地，恰当地
- stove /stəʊv/ *n.* 火炉，炉子
- torch /tɔːtʃ/ *n.* 手电筒
- trick /trɪk/ *v.* 欺骗，哄骗

Phrases & expressions 短语和表达

- at heart 本质上，内心里

- camping stove 野营炉
- light up 照亮，使发亮，使发光
- might as well 倒不如，不妨

Reading exercise 阅读练习

Match the beginnings and the endings.

1) Nick and Laura are staying
2) Laura goes outside
3) Nick finds Kip
4) Kip has eaten
5) Nick doesn't help Laura

_______ a) under a chair.
_______ b) some rat poison.
_______ c) in a barn.
_______ d) to find a vet.
_______ e) to look for Kip.

Chapter 5

New words 生词

- chest /tʃest/ *n.* 胸部
- jumper /ˈdʒʌmpə(r)/ *n.* 短上衣
- painful /ˈpeɪnfl/ *a.* 令人痛苦（或难过、难堪）的
- pullover /ˈpʊləʊvə(r)/ *n.* 套衫，套头毛衣
- tummy /ˈtʌmi/ *n.* 肚子（儿童化用语）
- veterinary /ˈvetrənəri/ *a.* 兽医的

Phrases & expressions 短语和表达

- in turn 依次，挨个
- it's up to sb. 取决于某人
- sit up 坐直
- wide of the mark 不着边际，离谱

Reading exercises 阅读练习

1. What is happening to Robert when he wakes up?
2. What does Robert think about city people?
3. How did Laura get to the vet's surgery?
4. Where did Laura see the vet before?
5. What does Robert offer to do with Kip that night?

Chapter 6

New words 生词

- bacon /ˈbeɪkən/ *n.* 腌猪肉，熏猪肉，培根
- company /ˈkʌmpəni/ *n.* 陪伴；同伴
- eyelash /ˈaɪlæʃ/ *n.* 睫毛
- mushroom /ˈmʌʃrʊm/ *n.* 蘑菇
- omelette /ˈɒmlət/ *n.* 煎蛋卷
- overnight /ˌəʊvəˈnaɪt/ *ad.* 在夜间
- receptionist /rɪˈsepʃənɪst/ *n.* 接待员
- sailing /ˈseɪlɪŋ/ *n.* 帆船运动
- vehicle /ˈviːəkl/ *n.* 车辆，交通工具

Reading exercises 阅读练习

1. Use adjectives to describe these things.
   a) What the morning is like.
   b) How Laura feels about jet-skis.
   c) The air in the countryside.
   d) The sound of the jet-skis.
   e) What Maggie thinks Robert might become.
   f) What Maggie looks like.
   g) How Robert often feels now that Chiara has gone.
   h) Robert thinks Laura has the dog because it's this.
   i) How Robert feels when Laura is not at the barn. (Two words)
2. What does Robert think about
   a) his receptionist Maggie?
   b) Laura?
   c) having a dog?
   d) jet-skiers?

Chapter 7

New words 生词

- arrange /əˈreɪndʒ/ *v.* 安排
- blackberry /ˈblækbəri/ *n.* 黑莓
- olive /ˈɒlɪv/ *n.* 橄榄
- pile /paɪl/ *n.* 堆；成堆的东西
- salami /səˈlɑːmi/ *n.* 意大利蒜味香肠

Phrases & expressions 短语和表达

- annoyed with... 对……厌烦
- cut up 切碎
- pack up 整理；打包
- voice mail 语音信箱

Reading exercise 阅读练习

True or false?

_______ a) Laura collected mushrooms in the fields.

_______ b) Nick came home for a long lunch.

_______ c) Nick wants to go water-skiing in the afternoon.

_______ d) Robert takes Kip to Nick first.

_______ e) Robert thinks that Nick and Laura are 'awful'.

_______ f) Laura has to pay Robert £200 for Kip's treatment.

_______ g) Laura thanks the vet for his work with Kip.

_______ h) The vet likes Nick and Laura.

Chapter 8

New words 生词

- audience /ˈɔːdiəns/ *n.* 观众；听众
- ceiling /ˈsiːlɪŋ/ *n.* 天花板
- dreamily /ˈdriːmɪli/ *ad.* 出神地
- noisily /ˈnɔɪzɪli/ *ad.* 吵闹地，喧闹地
- view /vjuː/ *n.* 景色，风景

Phrases & expressions 短语和表达

- drop off 让……下车
- get over（从不快或疾病中）恢复过来
- have no effect on... 对……没有影响
- have nothing to do with... 与……无关
- mess about 闲逛，消磨时间

Reading exercises 阅读练习

1. Who was Chiara?
2. How did she die?
3. Who were the jet-skiers?
4. How did Robert find out about Chiara's death?
5. The next morning, who
   a) wants to go for a walk?
   b) wants to go jet-skiing?
   c) wants to use the car?
   d) is upset by the story about Chiara?
   e) isn't sympathetic about Robert?
   f) needs to get some money?

Chapter 9

New words 生词

- depression /dɪˈpreʃn/ *n.* 抑郁
- interrupt /ˌɪntəˈrʌpt/ *v.* 打断，插嘴
- lean /liːn/ *v.*（身体）倾斜
- odd /ˈɒd/ *a.* 古怪的，不寻常的

- pony /ˈpəʊni/ *n.* 矮种马；小马
- psychologist /saɪˈkɒlədʒɪst/ *n.* 心理学家
- supplier /səˈplaɪə(r)/ *n.* 供应商

Phrases & expressions 短语和表达

- at the thought of... 一想到……（就）
- tell sb. off 训斥，责备

Cultural notes 文化点滴

- Cockermouth: 科克茅斯，英国城镇，位于英格兰坎布里亚郡。
- Labrador: 拉布拉多猎犬（简称“拉布拉多”），一种中大型犬类，天性温和、活泼，没有攻击性，智商高，适合被选作导盲犬或其他工作犬。

Reading exercise 阅读练习

What do you find out in this chapter about

a) Laura's feelings for Nick?

b) Laura's feelings about the countryside?

c) Maggie's feelings for Robert?

d) Laura's feelings for Robert?

e) Robert's feelings for Laura?

Chapter 10

New words 生词

- breech /briːtʃ/ *n.* 臀部；臀位

- calf /kɑːf/ *n.* 牛犊
- farmyard /ˈfɑːmjɑːd/ *n.* 农家庭院，农场
- lead /liːd/ *n.*（牵狗用的）皮带，链条，绳索
- moo /muː/ *v.* 发出哞哞声
- stuck /stʌk/ *a.* 被卡住的

Phrases & expressions 短语和表达

- let out 发出（声音）
- lie on one's side 侧躺着
- pull a face 板着脸；做鬼脸
- pull up（使车）慢慢停下
- turn out to be 结果是，原来是

Reading exercise 阅读练习

Put the events in the right order.

______ a) Laura leaves the farm to get Nick from the lake.

______ b) Robert tells the farmer that Laura is better than Nick.

______ c) Laura visits a farm to talk about buying cheese.

______ d) Maggie is surprised when Robert agrees to go to the pub with her.

______ e) Robert arrives at the farm too late to help.

______ f) Laura helps a calf to be born.

Chapter 11

New words 生词

- dull /dʌl/ *a.* 沉闷的，乏味的，无聊的

- Persian /ˈpɜːʃn/ *a.* 波斯的；波斯人的
- stool /stuːl/ *n.* 凳子

Phrases & expressions 短语和表达

- be attached to... 喜爱，依恋，对……有感情
- give birth 生孩子，产仔

Reading exercises 阅读练习

1. Where does the action of this scene take place?
2. Who is Barbara?
3. What does Barbara do?
4. Why is Barbara pleased about Robert?
5. Who says these things?
   a) 'It made me think my life's quite dull.'
   b) 'Then the vet isn't doing a very good job, is he?'
   c) 'I've had enough of all this local food.'
   d) '...there are people who like living alone better than sharing their house with anyone...'
   e) 'Robert saved Kip's life.'
   f) 'You're taking my work away from me.'
   g) 'If you'd like to visit my shop, I'd love to talk to you more.'

Chapter 12

New words 生词

- affect /əˈfekt/ *v.* 影响
- home-made /ˌhəʊmˈmeɪd/ *a.* 自制的，家里做的

- jar /dʒɑː(r)/ *n.* 罐，广口瓶
- lemonade /ˌleməˈneɪd/ *n.* 柠檬水
- oven /ˈʌvn/ *n.* 炉，灶；烤炉；烤箱

Phrases & expressions 短语和表达

- for now 目前，暂时
- hold on to... 保持，保留；抓牢
- take in 领会，理解

Cultural notes 文化点滴

- Coniston Lake: 科尼斯顿湖，英国湖区 16 个湖中的第三大湖。
- High Street: 城镇主要商业街通用的一个转喻说法，通常是市中心商店和商家最集中的地方，可以翻译为“商业街”，在英国及英联邦国家尤为常用。

Reading exercise 阅读练习

True or false?

_______ a) Nick decides not to go jet-skiing on Saturday.

_______ b) Laura drives to Cockermouth to meet Barbara.

_______ c) Laura realises she really loves Nick very much.

_______ d) Barbara and Laura get on very well.

_______ e) Barbara thinks Robert is very happy now.

_______ f) Barbara invites Laura to go walking with her that afternoon.

Chapter 13

New words 生词

- bad-tempered /ˌbædˈtempəd/ *a.* 脾气不好的，易怒的
- complicated /ˈkɒmplɪkeɪtɪd/ *a.* 难懂的，复杂的
- crossly /ˈkrɒsli/ *ad.* 发怒地
- embarrassed /ɪmˈbærəst/ *a.* 尴尬的，窘迫的
- pointless /ˈpɔɪntləs/ *a.* 无意义的
- sideways /ˈsaɪdweɪz/ *ad.* 向侧面地，向一旁

Phrases & expressions 短语和表达

- an armful of... 一抱……（东西）
- at heel 紧跟在后面
- fall away 消失，离开
- fall into place（开始）形成有条不紊、一目了然的格局，变得有条不紊（或清清楚楚）
- remind sb. of sth. 提醒某人某事
- up to a point 在一定程度上

Reading exercises 阅读练习

1. Who thinks these things, Nick or Laura?
   a) Kip is stupid.
   b) The vet is bad-tempered.
   c) The local people are important.
   d) Chiara's death was her own fault.
   e) Their relationship will end back in London.
2. What surprises Laura on the walk?

3. '"That's excellent," said Robert.' What is excellent?
4. What does Barbara say that helps Robert understand more about Laura?
5. What puzzles Robert about Laura?
6. What does Robert say that puzzles Laura?

Chapter 14

New words 生词

- breathless /ˈbreθləs/ *a.* 喘不过气来的
- corduroy /ˈkɔːdərɔɪ/ *n.* 灯芯绒
- mug /mʌg/ *n.* 圆筒形有柄大杯
- owe /əʊ/ *v.* 欠，应给予

Phrases & expressions 短语和表达

- apart from... 除……之外
- for certain 肯定地，确凿地
- French window 落地窗
- get going 出发，动身
- in time for... 及时赶上……
- sheets of rain 倾盆大雨

Reading exercise 阅读练习

Match the beginnings and the endings.

1) Barbara and Laura make arrangements
2) Barbara asks Laura
3) Robert invites Laura

4) Robert apologises to Laura
5) Laura agrees with Robert
6) Laura is starting to have

_______ a) into his house for a cup of tea.
_______ b) that jet-skis are horrible things.
_______ c) feelings for Robert.
_______ d) about sending food to London.
_______ e) for thinking that she was a bad person before.
_______ f) to give Robert a lift home.

Chapter 15

New words 生词

- head /hed/ *v.* 朝着……行进
- impatiently /ɪmˈpeɪʃntli/ *ad.* 不耐烦地，无耐性地

Phrases & expressions 短语和表达

- (be) different to... 与……不同
- fall for sb. 爱上某人，迷恋某人

Reading exercises 阅读练习

1. What does Laura realise about her feelings as she leaves Robert's house?
2. Who telephones Laura and why?
3. What does that mean for Kip?
4. How does Nick feel about Laura keeping the dog?
5. What idea does Laura have about Kip?

Chapter 16

New words 生词

- emptiness /ˈemptinəs/ *n.* 空虚，空洞
- platform /ˈplætfɔːm/ *n.* 月台，站台
- sigh /saɪ/ *v.* 叹息，叹气

Phrases & expressions 短语和表达

- be meant for 命中注定，注定要成为
- have...in common 与……有相同之处

Reading exercises 阅读练习

1. Answer the questions with short answers.
   a) Who wants to go home by train?
   b) Who wants to be with Laura?
   c) Who phones Laura?
   d) Who gets off the train?
   e) Who comes to meet Laura?
2. Who did Laura think Robert was going out with?
3. What doesn't happen as they drive by the lake?
4. What do Robert and Laura do at the end of the story?

Translation 参考译文

情定湖区

第 1 章　湖区

第5页

一声巨大的碰撞声，接着是一声长而响亮的尖叫，之后是一片寂静。

罗伯特开车穿过树林经过湖泊时，听见了撞击声和尖叫声。每天他都希望经过湖泊时不要发生这种情况，但这次又发生了。救护车的鸣笛声响起，蓝色的警灯不停地闪烁着。他开始害怕得颤抖起来。在他的左边，透过眼角的余光，他能够看到湖水被鲜血染红了。

他停下车，身体仍在发抖。他用双手抱着头。当他抬头向湖面望去时，那里什么也没有，压根儿就没发生过什么。

“这是为什么？为什么我开车经过这个地方时，同样的事情总是一次又一次地发生？”他恼怒地想着。

恢复平静后，他启动车子，慢慢驶向酒馆。

回家的路上罗伯特经常在那个地方停下待一会儿，在那里吃饭比工作了漫长的一天后自己做饭要轻松些。酒馆的食物很可口，是本地自产的有机食品。但罗伯特更喜欢在酒馆里吃饭的真正原因是，这样他就可以在自己的房子里少待一些时间，那个如今冷冷清清的房子。

第6页

今晚他想早点儿睡。他是名兽医，得随叫随到。他希望在电话铃声响起之前，尽可能多睡一会儿。每年的这个时候也的确会有几个夜晚他没被人叫醒，但经常有人需要他，也许有绵羊或奶牛生病了。春季里电话总是响个不停。绵羊产崽，他整夜不能睡。这些是重要的电话——来自劳作的农民，他们需要这些牲畜。然而，也有些人在没有必要的时候打来电话。

举个例子，前几天费洛斯夫人曾在午夜打电话给罗伯特，因为她的猫——哈里一直打喷嚏。这真的不算是紧急情况，但费洛斯夫人非常担心，所以罗伯特起床去了诊所。

罗伯特告诉费洛斯夫人哈里只是感冒了，它非常健康。但费洛斯夫人说起她的猫来一直说到凌晨一点多钟。罗伯特边听边点头，心里在想："其实有病的不是您的猫，而是您自己，费洛斯夫人。"

第7页

不过他什么也没说，他理解费洛斯夫人很孤独。是费洛斯夫人需要他，而不是那只猫。

当地人认为罗伯特是一个善良的人，总是愿意倾听。近来他不怎么说话，不过这没关系。大家喜欢他安静的面容，以及他为大家付出的时间。他们叫他"沉默的兽医"。他们对他的私生活很好奇，但没人问过。

现在罗伯特驶离了湖边，到达那条穿过树林的笔直道路时，他踩下了油门。每年的这个时候，他很少碰到其他车辆。游客大多已离去，而九月晚上的这个时间当地人都已回到了家里。他驶出树林，尽量去想正在等待他的美食。他尽量不去想湖泊，不去想骑水上摩托艇的人，不去想夕阳西下时慢慢泛红的湖水。

第2章 伦敦

第8页

砰，砰，砰！砰，砰，砰！

劳拉睁开眼睛，看到窗外蓝色的警灯不停地闪烁着。她坐了起来，感到惊慌。外面仍是一片漆黑。有人在砰砰地大声敲她的门。

她打开床头灯，看了看时钟，是凌晨两点钟。谁会在这个时间敲她的门呢？

她匆忙穿上便袍和拖鞋，跑去打开前门。一名救护车司机正站在那儿。

“我很抱歉在晚上这个时候叫醒您。”他说。

“发生什么事了……是谁……？”劳拉说不下去了。她的心跳得很快。

“您的邻居，约瑟夫·唐纳森——我们要送他去医院。我们认为他是心脏病发作了。”救护车司机说。

“哦，天哪！我能帮上什么忙吗？”劳拉问道。

约瑟夫是住在隔壁的一位老人。劳拉非常喜欢他，并且经常帮助他。但是他年纪大了，心脏不好已经很久了。她不得不承认她很庆幸是约瑟夫，而不是她自己的家人或朋友生病了。

第9页

“能，”救护车司机说，“我就是来问这个的。是有关他的狗。约瑟夫说您提出过如果他发生了意外，您会照看他的狗。他希望在自己住院期间由您来照看他的狗。”

“哦，没问题。我这就来。”劳拉说。

几分钟后，劳拉站在约瑟夫的起居室里，怀中抱着一只小狗。

她看着救护车的医护人员把约瑟夫抬了出去。

老人抬头看着劳拉。

“你会照看它的，对吗?”他说。劳拉握住约瑟夫的手。

“您别担心，”她说，“我会照看它的，我保证。”

“因为我不想基普死在我前面。”老人说。

“哦，不，我相信它不会的。”劳拉和善地说，然后突然怀疑这是不是该说的话。

“我的意思是……”她继续说，“您瞧，你们俩谁都不会死。您会没事的，我会照看基普直到您回家。”

第10页

“谢谢你，亲爱的。你是个好姑娘。”约瑟夫说，之后他就被抬走了。

救护车开走了，劳拉怀里抱着小狗看着车离开。

然后她想起件事。“我今天下午要和尼克去湖区！关于这只狗他会说什么呢?”她心想。

她想起了尼克对她说的话：“我通常一个人去。我喜欢回归大地，做一些水上运动等。但我不想过四天没有你的日子。不知道你愿不愿意一起去?”

劳拉当时说：“好！好，我当然愿意去！”

在湖区待四天！而且是和尼克在一起！

她只是几周前才遇到他。有一天，他走进她的商店兼咖啡馆，点了一杯卡布奇诺。然后第二天和之后的一天他也来了，这时劳拉开始琢磨这个时髦、有趣的男人是谁。

她和她商店里的助手乔经常就她们的顾客玩猜谜游戏，猜测他们的名字、职业和性情。商店里清静无客人时，这是一个打发时间的好方法，这个游戏让她们开怀大笑。

第11页

“你觉得他是做什么工作的？”有一天劳拉问乔。

尼克刚刚离开商店。他当时身穿一件皮夹克和时髦的保罗·史密斯牌衬衫。

“我觉得他是个银行经理。”乔说。

“哦，不是！”劳拉说，“他比银行经理更有文艺气质。”

“时装设计师？”乔建议道。

“不，我想他可能是个善于交际的人——也许是老师？”劳拉说。

“太时髦了！医生？”乔说。

“不，神情太悠闲。或许他是个电影导演？”劳拉说。

“对，名叫弗朗西斯科的导演！”乔笑着说。

“迈尔斯。”劳拉说。

“好，迈尔斯。”乔赞同道，“他导演恐怖片，闲暇时他常去攀岩。而且他喜欢你，劳拉。”

“嗯，”劳拉说，“我很喜欢爱攀岩的电影导演这个想法！”乔和劳拉都笑了起来。

尼克终于约劳拉出去了。他说他在劳拉的咖啡馆附近工作，是一名设计师。他住在一栋高档的新公寓里。他骑摩托车，还有一辆跑车。他告诉劳拉，他喜欢赛车。

第12页

“不是攀岩？”劳拉问他，她的眼睛闪闪发亮。

“不，我不喜欢爬高。”尼克回答，“你为什么会这么问？”

“没什么，”她说，“我只是好奇。”

他们开始经常见面。劳拉喜欢和他在一起。他们去泰晤士河旁边高档的餐馆和酒吧，他给她讲一些让她大笑的故事。

而现在他邀请她和他一起去湖区，那里是英格兰她最喜欢的地方之一，是英格兰最适合散步的地方之一。所以他不仅仅是个城市人，他也喜欢乡村！这点对劳拉而言很重要，有很重要的意义。

劳拉回到床上，让基普躺在床尾，她感到困惑。

"如果尼克不想让狗去，或许我将只能待在这里，"她心想，"我答应过约瑟夫会照看基普，我不能让他失望。"

她想想四天独自一人与一只狗待在公寓里，又想想与尼克一起待在湖区。她知道自己更喜欢哪一个。她喜欢乡下。也许……也许她开始爱上尼克了，她不确定。她已经好久没有喜欢上、真正喜欢上一个人了。

第13页

"好吧。"她对自己笑了笑。"他终究不是一名电影导演，但他聪明、有趣，我的确喜欢和他在一起……而且我真的想和他一起去湖区。那么关于这只狗他会说些什么呢？"

第3章　狗也来了

第14页

"一只狗？"他问。

"对，一只狗！"

"那只狗？"

"对，这只狗。"

周四下午四点钟，尼克开着他的跑车来到了劳拉的公寓。他们俩约定周五休息。

劳拉站在打开的门旁，怀里抱着一只小狗。它长着长长的耳朵和长长的毛，颜色和尼克刚刚用来重新装饰自己公寓的漂亮油漆的颜色一样。这种油漆被称为“博恩”。

“我们不会带着一只狗去湖区的！”尼克说。

“对不起，”劳拉说，“昨晚约瑟夫进了医院，他心脏病发作了。所以我必须照看这只狗。如果它不能和我们一起去，我恐怕根本就去不成。”

“约瑟夫？约瑟夫是谁？”尼克问。

“你知道的，就是我跟你提起过的那位老人，他是我的邻居——我的朋友。”劳拉解释说。

“哦，是他！”尼克此刻想起来了。劳拉经常提起一位她有时去探望的老人。尼克当时听的时候没太在意。毕竟，这位老人七十六岁了。尼克对七十六岁的老男人不是很感兴趣。

第15页

“他没有其他人可以求助了吗？”尼克建议道。

“没有，尼克，”劳拉说，“你记得吧，我告诉过你他的妻子去年去世了。没有其他人能照看这只狗。”

“他没有孩子……孙子吗？”尼克继续说。

“没有，他只有我。”劳拉说。

尼克用舌头发出“啧啧”的声响。他一直盼望着周末在湖上玩摩托艇。然后他决定邀请劳拉一同前往。通常他从不邀请他的女朋友和他一起去。

而现在她要带上一只狗！正常情况下他会很生气。但当他看着金发蓬乱、脸颊粉红、怀抱小狗的劳拉时，他情不自禁地在想她看上去多么迷人。

“你啊，”尼克边说边走到劳拉身后，亲吻她的发丝，“太善良了，这就是你的问题。所以我们要带着一只狗一起度假……好吧，我想这会……很有趣。”

第16页

劳拉微笑着看着他说：“你的意思是基普也能一起去？”

“只是因为如果它不去，你就不会去，而我想你和我在一起。”尼克说。

“哦，真是太棒了！我太期待这个周末了！”劳拉说。

“好。好了，我们出发吧。”尼克说，“你的行李收拾好了吗？”

“一切都准备好了。”劳拉说着指了指前门旁边的两个包。

“现在，我们要把狗放在哪儿呢？”尼克问。

“它可以跟我坐在一起。”劳拉建议。

“这样允许吗？它必须到后面去，待在行李上面。”尼克说。

* * *

“我觉得我们需要停车。”劳拉说。

这时是四个小时之后了。尼克和劳拉已经离开伦敦，正驾车北上。

“什么？”尼克问。

“尼克，我们必须停车！基普需要出去一下。”劳拉说。

基普坐在他们的行李上面。这辆小跑车塞得满满的，里面有劳拉的两个包、尼克昂贵的皮制手提箱和潜水衣。

现在这只狗正在叫。尼克看上去很生气。

“尼克，我是为你的行李着想。”劳拉说。

第17页

“好吧，好吧。”尼克说。他把车停在路边，但是为了一只狗而停车他显然不悦。

“我们到那儿的时候得半夜了。”他说。

“对不起。”劳拉带着基普回到车里时说。

如果这只狗妨碍她进一步了解尼克，她会很不开心的。但是她能怎么办呢？她不得不帮助可怜的老约瑟夫。

他们再次出发时她快速看了尼克一眼。他生她的气了吗？他看了看她，然后笑了。他拿起她的手握住。她悬着的心放了下来。

“一切都会好的，”她心想，“也许尼克甚至会学着爱上这只狗。”

* * *

一个半小时后，尼克在一家酒馆外面放慢车速。

“我们为什么要停车？”劳拉问。

“我们需要吃饭。我们现在快到地方了，而且我真的饿了！”

“但是我包里有食物，我从店里带了一些东西。我们到地方后，我可以做饭。”

劳拉感到失望。做饭是她的一大爱好。她一直期盼这个周末能为尼克做饭。在湖区的这段时间，她还想为他们其余的几顿饭寻找当地的好食材。

第18页

“我只是不确定厨房是什么样子。”尼克说。劳拉觉得他看起来相当内疚。

“你是什么意思？”她问。

“就是厨房可能不是非常现代化。”尼克答道，“不管怎样，我想请你吃晚餐。你已经工作整整一个星期了，这是你应得的。”

他们停下来吃饭的那家酒馆温馨而热情，尽管这里几乎是空无一人。

劳拉和尼克坐在壁炉附近的一个角落里。他们的桌子上摆放着花。在酒馆里能闻到柴火的烟味和美食的香气。他们仔细看了菜单，然后选了食物。

“还不错。”劳拉边说边吃一块鸡肉馅饼和沙拉。不管走到哪里，她都喜欢品尝当地的食物。她总是留意新的东西，以便在她的咖啡馆出售。尼克正在吃野鸡。

“挺好的，这是当地的有机食物，你不觉得吗？”劳拉说。

“是不错，不过我可以来一份美味的泰式绿咖喱。”尼克说，劳拉开玩笑地打了他一下。

基普坐在桌子下面。劳拉喂了它一些鸡肉渣。

第19页

吧台那里坐着一名个子高挑、头发凌乱的男子。劳拉看了看他。这人看起来蛮有意思的，她心想，长着一张聪明的脸却一脸忧伤。

第20页

关于他，乔会说些什么呢？一位诗人，她可能会这么猜。像华兹华斯那样的山间诗人？

那名男子没有看他俩，尽管房间里除了他俩再无旁人。要说有什么的话，劳拉倒是发觉，他似乎在回避他们。

“这附近的人不是很友善，”尼克说，“我之前以为北方人总是很友好。”

“嗯，这只是一个人，”劳拉说，“你不能因为一个人的行为而对所有的北方人下定论。”

“但是这里没有其他人，为什么他不跟我们打招呼呢？”

“也许他不喜欢游客。”劳拉说，并开始在脑海中勾勒这名男子的画面。她能看到他在雨中翻越一道道山冈，然后回到小小的家中，借着炉火之光写下忧伤的诗句。他有可能很穷，因为作家从来没有挣大钱的。

“你觉得他是一位诗人吗？”她问尼克。

“谁？”尼克问。

“吧台那儿的那个人。”劳拉说。

“一位诗人？我不知道，”尼克说，“他看起来很不友好。这就是我能看到的。你为什么问这个？”

“哦，没什么。”劳拉说。“瞧，我累了，”她说，“我们去房子那儿好吗？”

第21页

“房子？”尼克重复道。

“我们要住的地方。”劳拉说。

“哦，那个啊！好，我们走吧。”尼克答道。

第 4 章　中毒！

第22页

“谷仓？农舍？”劳拉问道。

“是的，谷仓！”尼克回答说。

“但是……但是我原以为你是那种习惯洗热水澡、用柔软毛巾的男人。”劳拉说。

“对，我是，我在伦敦时是这样，”尼克说，“但在乡村时，我喜欢乡村的生活方式。”

“你是说乡村人全都住在冰冷的谷仓里吗？”劳拉笑着问道。

“我是说，一个人有时放弃舒适的城市生活是有好处的。”

“这也许对男人而言是件好事，”劳拉说，“但我不确定对我这个女人，或者这只可怜的小狗来说也是件好事！”

他们把车停在一栋高大的石头房子门外。此时已是晚上 11 点钟。他们推开门时，劳拉简直不敢相信自己的眼睛。他们倒不如说是露营呢！这里有灯，但没什么别的东西了。没有暖气，没有电视，没有洗澡的地方。有一个小厨房，里面有个可以做饭的野营用的炉子。几级木制楼梯的顶部有几张床。屋子里很冷。

第23页

基普穿过大屋子跑进一个小一些的侧间。劳拉走进厨房。

“尼克，你为什么不告诉我我们要住在谷仓里？”劳拉问道。

“因为，”他边说边搂住她，“我怕如果我告诉了你，你就不来了。”

“嗯，你说对了！”劳拉说。

尼克笑了。“但你现在在这儿了，”他说，“而且回家的路很远。”

劳拉也笑了，任由他把自己拉向他身边。“这么说你是骗我和你一起来的啊。”她说。

“你也骗我带了一只狗来呀。”他答道。

“是的。”她微笑着说道。他吻了她。

“我最好去看看基普。”劳拉说。

尼克装出伤心的样子。“我希望你不要开始喜欢那只狗胜过喜欢我！”他说。

“嘿！”劳拉说，“你不是一个无依无靠没有妈妈的动物！我只是要去看看……”

“你需要一个手电筒，”尼克说，“那间屋子里没有电。给你。”

劳拉穿过冰冷的谷仓。她感到很吃惊，尼克竟然选了这个谷仓来度假。他看起来不像是那种喜欢野营的人——你越了解一个人，他们展现出来的东西就越有趣。但她感到很开心，看起来他比自己之前想的更有趣。虽然她之前和尼克开玩笑，但她实际上酷爱野营。她喜欢在野营炉上做饭这个主意，她喜欢坐在真实的火堆旁取暖！“我本质上是一个乡下姑娘，”她心想，“这么看来，我和尼克比我想象的更相似！”

第24页

她拿起羊毛外套裹在身上，拿着手电筒走向侧间。她打开门，用手电筒在房间里照了一圈，没看到基普！

有扇门通向花园。劳拉发觉门没关好。基普是出去了吗？她推开门。

“基普！基普！”她大声喊道。她走到外面，用手电筒照了照四周，手电筒照亮了灌木丛和树丛。

劳拉的心跳开始加快。她往树林深处走去。

“基普！基普！你在哪儿？”她喊道。她开始担心起来。或许它迷路了，或许一只大一些的动物把它吃了。狐狸吃狗吗？她不知道。

第25页

基普发生了什么事？如果弄丢了它，她该怎么办？如果约瑟夫知道基普遭遇了不测，他会很伤心，也许好不起来了！她知道他有多么爱他的小狗。

她在树林里站了几分钟，一直喊着“基普！基普！”，但没有回应。

"我还是回去吧，"劳拉心想，"尼克会好奇我在哪儿。"她转身向谷仓走去。

"劳拉！劳拉！你在哪里？"尼克在叫她。

"在外面这儿，在找基普。"她回应道。

"它在这儿呢！"尼克喊道。

劳拉以最快的速度穿过树林往回走。尼克站在门口，也拿着一把手电筒。

"它在椅子下面，"劳拉回来时他说，"但我觉得它可能有点儿不对劲。"

劳拉弯下腰摸了摸小狗。它没有动，也没有睁眼。

第26页

"嘿，你看！这是什么？"尼克问。他的手电筒照到地板上一个打开的盒子里的一些粉末上。

"这是什么？"劳拉说着捡起了盒子。

她的心猛然一跳。盒子上写着"鼠药"。

"哦，天哪！尼克，它吃了这个吗？"劳拉喊道。

"看起来它的嘴边沾了些粉末。"尼克回答。

"哦！我们该怎么办？"劳拉喊道。

"我们没什么能做的。"尼克说。

"我答应过约瑟夫。我答应过约瑟夫会照看它。它会死吗，尼克？"劳拉说。

"我不知道。"尼克说。

"但是如果基普死了，约瑟夫可能会死……听我说，我们需要带它看兽医。"劳拉说。

"劳拉，现在快半夜了！"尼克说。

"一定有急诊兽医的，就像有急诊医生一样。"劳拉说。

她把基普抱在膝盖上。它看起来病得不轻。

"劳拉，"尼克说，"我们只在这里单独待四个晚上，我才不会花掉其中一个晚上为一只甚至不是我们的动物找兽医的！"

"我不能让约瑟夫失望。"劳拉说。她再次把手放在小狗的身体旁，它摸上去凉凉的。

第27页

"它病得很重。"她说，她现在是真的害怕了，"这是我的错。我们必须做点儿什么！"

劳拉看着尼克。为什么他不明白她不是愿意这样做，而是不得不这样做？她不得不这样做，因为她答应过约瑟夫。

尼克看起来很生气。"我要去睡觉了，"他说，"开了一路车我累了。明天我想早起。"

尼克上了楼，留下劳拉一个人抱着基普。她几乎要哭了。不过这是为小狗担心的眼泪，还是对尼克失望的眼泪呢？她不确定。

第5章　急诊

第28页

又是一声巨响，一声尖叫。灯光闪烁。鲜血浸染了水面。

罗伯特醒了。他的心狂跳不止，但屋里一片漆黑。又是那个梦，每天晚上都是同一个梦。这梦就像是一次次重新经历那个可怕的夜晚。可那已经是整整两年前的事情了。为什么这梦不能停下来呢？

他坐起来，看了看表，正是午夜。几秒钟后，他意识到电话铃声在响。他拿起电话。

“急诊。一只狗中毒了。”一个声音说道。是他的急救电话中心打来的。

罗伯特写下一个名字，仍半睡半醒。他穿上裤子和一件宽大的套头衫，动身去诊所。

通常情况下，打急救电话的人，他们的宠物都没什么问题，就像费洛斯夫人的猫一样。罗伯特喜欢动物，但动物的需求与人的不同，它们并非每次感冒都需要兽医。

第29页

罗伯特一边开车一边想，最糟糕的是那些夏天来这儿度假的城里人，他们穿着丑陋无比、颜色鲜艳的衣服来到这儿，整个湖区都充斥着他们喧闹的水上运动。通常，他们会带上狗甚至是猫。有时他们的狗在山上追赶绵羊，农民们对此十分生气。

但罗伯特不喜欢城里人的真正原因更令人痛心，他拒绝谈论此事。

路上没有其他车辆。他开车时尽量不去想两年前的那个晚上，他需要保持冷静。

他花了十分钟到达诊所。他跳下车，推开诊所的门，打开灯。他把一些干净的纸放在桌子上，准备好一些东西。一只狗中毒了，这就是他所知道的一切。

* * *

劳拉不喜欢夜里这个时候独自在漆黑的路上开车。但是尽管她再次询问尼克是否愿意和她一起去，他还是拒绝了。

第30页

“如果你愿意的话可以把车开走，”他说，“但我要睡觉。你自己看着办吧，你可以和我在这儿待着，也可以带狗去看兽医。但我哪儿都不去。”

她感到害怕，她沿着空荡荡的漆黑的乡村公路开着车，经过湖泊，然后穿过树林，爬上另一座小山，她希望自己是按照她在电话中被告知的路线行驶。

她希望尼克和她在一起去。她之前对他感到失望，但是现在，开着车，她有了不同的想法。

“他说过他通常不带任何人和他一起来湖区的，”她心想，“他当然不会想到我会带一只狗来。他不想花费一整夜时间寻找兽医，这真的并不出人意料。”

当她在一个小屋外面停下车时，已近凌晨一点了。屋子上方清楚地写着“兽医诊所”。屋里亮着灯，因此她知道一定是这里了。

基普躺在汽车前座上，身上盖着劳拉的套衫和外套保暖。劳拉托着它的小身体下了车，急匆匆地走到门口按门铃。门开了。

劳拉不确定她会见到什么样的人，可能是一位头发灰白、戴着眼镜的中年人。恰恰相反，她立刻认出这个男人就是当天晚上早些时候在酒馆的那个人。她愚蠢地想：“可你是一位诗人啊！”

第31页

他穿着一件旧套头衫，金黄色的头发没有梳理。如此看来，他是一名兽医，而非诗人！她先前的猜测太离谱了！要不是基普病得这么重，她也许会发笑。

“你认为它中毒了？”兽医边问边从劳拉的怀里接过基普。

“是的，我把它放在了一个地上有老鼠药的房间里。”劳拉说。

“你带来一些没有？”兽医问道。

“没有。”劳拉说。

“把狗留在房间里之前你没有检查房间吗？”兽医问。

“没有。我们刚到这里。从伦敦开车到这儿需要六小时，我累了，我没想到……我没想到地上会有老鼠药。”劳拉说。

“你们住在哪儿？”兽医问。

“我们露营……”劳拉告诉他。

“你们露营？”兽医说。

“嗯，类似露营——在一个谷仓里。”劳拉解释说。

“在谷仓里露营？”兽医说。

第32页

劳拉希望他不要一直重复自己说的每句话，这让她觉得自己很愚蠢。他仍然没有笑。总之，他的头发遮住了大半张脸，所以她不知道他在想什么。

然后他沉默不语了，似乎沉默了很长很长时间。

罗伯特不说话了，他感到气愤。“他们就是这个样子，”他想，“到湖区来的人不知道如何在乡村生活。你住在谷仓里，所以你不想有老鼠，当然会用老鼠药。如果你有狗，你首先得检查住所。”

劳拉看着。他的大手摸了摸狗的小胸口和肚子，然后依次捏起它的每只耳朵闻了闻。

“你住的那个地方在哪里？”他问。

“在贝克斯托尔·费尔，就像一个……嗯，只是一个有几张床的谷仓。里面非常冷，那里显然有老鼠，但是……”她意识到他没有真的在听。

“我需要给狗吃点药。”他说。

“它会没事吧？”劳拉问。

“我想我们可能还算及时。”兽医答道。他快速看了她一眼说：

“你给我打电话是对的，要不然它可能会死。”

第33页

兽医给狗吃药时，劳拉坐在一旁看着。“为什么我没有检查谷仓里有没有毒药呢？”她心想，“我不习惯养狗，我没有考虑到基普的安全。”

她看着兽医，他的大手轻柔地在狗的身上移动着。她心想，他的脸上尽管没有笑容，却是一张温和的脸。但是她又一次注意到他身上流露出的深深的忧伤。

现在基普睁开了眼睛，它看起来好一些了。

“你刚才说是一个谷仓，那里有暖气吗？有热水吗？”兽医问。

“没有，那里很简陋。”劳拉说。

“那这样吧。”他说。他终于站直了身子看着她，并把头发从眼前拨开，现在她看到了，他的眼睛是蓝色的。“今晚我把这只狗带回我家。让它暖和些比较好。”

劳拉很吃惊。她既惊讶又感激，都想吻他了。这似乎太体贴了，本没必要这么体贴的。但她能看得出，无论你多么感激，他都不是那种你可以亲吻的男人。

第34页

“谢谢你，”她转而说道，“非常感谢你。你一定认为我太笨了，没有先检查谷仓，但是……”

“我明天会把它带给你。地址是哪里？”兽医问。

劳拉告诉了兽医谷仓在哪里，他点了点头。

“我知道这个地方，”他说，“反正我明天要去那边见一个农民。我上午会把狗带过去，如果它的情况好些的话。”

“你真是太好了，”劳拉回答说，“我感觉好多了。我之前很担心，不知道该做什么。”

劳拉终于感到开心了，基普会没事的。她转身要离开。

“嗯……”她刚走出门，兽医就开口说。她转过身来。

“我忘问了——它叫什么名字？”兽医说。

“谁的名字？”劳拉问。

兽医看着她，仿佛她疯了，接着他摸了摸小狗的头。

“哦……哦，抱歉，”劳拉说，“它叫基普。”

“好，晚安。”他说。

劳拉再次在夜色中出发了，感觉比来时的路上好多了。

第 6 章　在湖上

第35页

第二天早上尼克走进厨房。劳拉正在用小野营炉煎培根。

“闻起来不错。”他说。

“给。”劳拉递给他一个盘子。“或许在尼克去做水上运动之前，我们可以去散散步。”她琢磨着。

而尼克另有主意。还没等劳拉坐下，他已迅速吃完早餐。

“好了！”他大声说，“我感觉好多了。现在，我们动身吧！”

“这就走？”劳拉问。

“我不想浪费任何时间，”尼克说，“这是一个美好的早晨，趁着天气好，我想去湖上。你要来吗？”

“我……我不确定。你要做什么水上运动？我相当喜欢帆船运动，但我不知道是否……”

“骑摩托艇。”尼克说。

“摩托艇？”劳拉看着他。她为什么会吃惊？尼克喜欢速度快的交通工具，他喜欢摩托车和跑车，所以他当然喜欢骑摩托艇。

第36页

“你要来吗？”他问道。

“不，不，我不去了，我从没玩过摩托艇。说实话，我有点儿害怕。你必须开得很快才行。”

“这就是乐趣所在！”尼克说，“不过别担心，我乐意一个人去，我可以回来和你一起吃午饭。”

“好吧。我和你一起到湖边，然后走回来。我也需要一些锻炼。”劳拉说。

尼克没有问起基普。昨晚劳拉回来时他已经睡着了。难道他忘记她在半夜去看兽医了吗？

“兽医把狗留在他那儿过夜了，”他们开车走着时劳拉说，“他担心它会在谷仓里受寒。”

“他还挺好心的。”尼克说，“那么，它还好吗？”

“是的，他人还行，有点儿少言寡语。”劳拉回答。

“不，我指的是狗。”尼克说着笑了。

“哦！哦，是的，基普很好。但幸好我去了，兽医说它差点儿就死了。”

“嘿，快看那个。”尼克说，没有回应劳拉。一艘鲜黄色的摩托艇正背着阳光在水面上飞驰。“我很快就要那样了！”

“酷。”劳拉说，突然意识到她真的对摩托艇没有一点儿兴趣。

第37页

他们沿着小路行驶时——就是她昨晚深夜走的那些路——劳拉

觉得乡村是那么美。高大的山峦耸立在路的两侧，在九月阳光的照耀下呈现出迷人的紫色和红色。道路转向一片银色水域，就是那片湖泊。劳拉情不自禁地想到摩托艇是湖面上唯一丑陋的东西。

在水上运动中心，尼克跳下车去和一个人聊天。

劳拉坐在车里，不知道自己为什么会在那儿。尼克几乎像是忘记了她，现在他要做他酷爱的事情——骑上一艘摩托艇。但是公平地说，他之前告诉过她，他通常不邀请女朋友来。或许是这个原因，他知道自己会很忙。

"那我就做自己喜欢的事吧。"她心想。

"午餐时见。"尼克回到车边说。

"好吧，"她说，"我会给你做午餐。待会儿见。"

她不知道自己为什么感到失望。她期望的是什么呢？期待他们俩整个周末都坐在咖啡馆里过浪漫的二人世界吗？

第38页

"不，"她心想，"我知道不会是那样的。但是花些时间一起散散步会挺好的。这是一个如此美丽的早晨。"

她沿着寂静的道路往回走，心里想着，这是自他们来到这里后她第二次独自一人走在这些路上。

田野里长满了蘑菇，在晨光中显得白嫩嫩的。她想采一些，午餐做一个美味十足的蘑菇煎蛋卷。

她回到谷仓，拿了一个大碗，动身前往最近的小山去采蘑菇。如果待在谷仓附近，她就能听到兽医的车。

"我希望基普没事了，"她心想，"它回来和我在一起我会更开心的。"

乡间的味道和新鲜的空气让她想起了自己的孩提时代。她是在农村长大的，经常怀念那里。然而，在农村没有像在伦敦一样的机会。她的商店和咖啡馆经营得不错，她现在不能离开它们。

“不知道我还能不能再次快乐地生活在像这样的地方。”她边走边想。

第39页

然后她意识到有什么东西不对。乡村的宁静正在被打破。是那恼人的摩托艇的声音，它们在湖上绕了一圈又一圈。

* * *

兽医的接待员玛吉正坐在她的办公桌旁，照着一面小镜子，检查自己的妆容。

“哦，多可爱的小宝贝！”看到罗伯特怀里的狗，她叫道。

“啊，它真可爱！是谁的？谁是你幸运的妈咪呀？”她边说边用手抚摸基普的头，然后抬头看着罗伯特。

“你一会儿要来白牛酒馆吗？”她问他。

“抱歉，玛吉。”罗伯特说。

她朝罗伯特甜甜一笑，希望他会注意到自己的长睫毛。

“你需要多出门，你知道的，”她说，“你越来越无聊了。如果你不小心点儿的话，你会变成一个无聊的老头儿的。”

罗伯特看着他的接待员，淡淡地笑了一下。她很善良，真的很善良，而且很迷人。她知道这一点！但他不想花一个晚上的时间和玛吉待在一起，听她谈论来诊所就诊的每一只宠物。她说他越来越无聊，但她自己也不是最有趣的同伴。

第40页

“我现在要出去，”他告诉玛吉，“我得去看看农民安斯沃思家的奶牛，还要顺路把这只狗还给它的主人。”

罗伯特爬进他的路虎车，低头看了看趴在身旁座位上的基普。他不得不承认自己十分喜欢这种类型的狗。自从基娅拉离世后，他经常感到孤独，但他没办法开始与另一个人分享他的生活。那样会太痛心。也许可以养一只狗？他想到了附近的农场。他们不需要更多的狗跑来跑去，追咬绵羊。驾车驶往谷仓时，这些想法萦绕在他的脑海里。

基普用两只前爪抵着车窗，立起身子望着窗外。突然它看见田野里有一只兔子，它上蹿下跳，狂吠不止。不行，有一只狗在身边的话，要想努力工作挺难的。

罗伯特到达谷仓时，看见那里没有汽车。“真不敢相信！她竟然出去了！她希望我把狗留在一个没人的谷仓里。”他心想。

第41页

他走出路虎，关上车门。他走到谷仓门前。如他所料，门锁着。里面没人。

“我告诉过那个女人我今天会来，”他心想，“她在哪儿呢？她看起来不像是那种会忘记自己的狗的女人。她似乎很担心它！”

他又绕着谷仓走了一圈，只是为了确定这里没人。然后他记起她说过他们是从伦敦来的。他感到非常恼火，开始发抖。

“她很可能每天出去工作时，就把这只可怜的小狗独自留在一套小公寓里，”他心想，“对她而言，这样做很正常！她养狗只是为了赶时髦。”

出于某种原因，他对这个女人感到既失望又生气。他把路虎车掉头，驱车返回，基普依然在他身边。

“我要去农民安斯沃思家，晚些时候再来。”他心想。

第42页

当他要开到主干道上时，他看见了那辆黄色的跑车。他认出那就是那个女人昨晚开的车。车停在湖边。他能看见骑摩托艇的人在湖上一圈又一圈地飞驰着，在水面上留下银白色的图案。玩摩托艇的人没有看见他。这么多噪声，他们不可能听见汽车声。他们在水面上飞驰，然后突然转弯，腾空而起。罗伯特感到愤怒，近乎身体疼痛一样的愤怒。

他意识到其中一个骑摩托艇的人一定是那辆车的主人。这么说基普的主人正在那儿玩摩托艇，而不是在谷仓等自己的狗！他再次感到莫名的失望。

“什么样的女人会对玩摩托艇比对自己的狗的身体状况更感兴趣呢？”他心想。

他动身前往农民安斯沃思家时，仍然感到生气。为什么还允许在湖面上玩摩托艇？没有什么东西比这些人给湖区带来的危险更让他生气和不快的了。

第 7 章　气话

第44页

劳拉采了足够多的蘑菇来做一顿美味可口的煎蛋卷。田野里还有黑莓，她也摘了一些。回到谷仓，她做了一份沙拉，切了一些火腿和萨拉米香肠，开了一罐橄榄。

她把盘子和玻璃杯放在桌子上，等着尼克玩完摩托艇后回来。

她看了看手表。将近两点了！劳拉简直不敢相信。那个兽医不是说今天上午会把基普送回来吗？

劳拉再次开始担心起来。如果基普最终没有好转怎么办？如果毒药真的伤到它了呢？

听见汽车开来的声音，她赶紧跑到外面看是不是兽医。她走向大门，看见是尼克开着跑车飞驰而来。

他跳下车。“真是太棒了！”他说，“我好饿。听我说，亲爱的，我今天下午想去滑水。我在那儿遇到一个人，他有小船和滑水板，所以我就简单吃点儿午饭，然后我就走了。你还好吗？”

第45页

“我很好。”劳拉说，给他看她做的午餐。“但我不知道基普在哪儿。兽医说上午会把它送回来。我希望狗没事。”

尼克坐了下来，吃着桌子上的食物。然后，他满嘴塞着食物向门口走去。

“嘿！”劳拉说，“我正在做煎蛋卷……”

“煎蛋卷？”尼克说，“没事儿。我现在不想吃别的东西了。我会在六点钟左右回来。我们可以去那家酒馆吃晚饭，你就不用做饭了。”

他在门外停下脚步，又走回屋里来到劳拉身边。

“嘿！”他说，“亲一个。”

劳拉站在门口，看着他开着跑车再次消失。

她回到桌子旁边，桌上摆满了好吃的东西。她看着准备好用来做煎蛋卷的那一堆蘑菇。

“我要怎么处理这些食物呢？”她困惑地想，“我要如何度过下午的剩余时间呢？基普怎么样了？”

第46页

此刻她感觉真的不开心，于是她找到手机，拨了兽医的号码。她的心跳得很快，但兽医的电话转接到了语音信箱。

“我是劳拉·巴顿，”她说，“我的狗基普在你那里。它怎么样了？我很担心，因为你今天上午没来。你收到这条信息后可以给我回个电话吗？”她留下了自己的手机号码。

劳拉感到孤独、悲伤，而且很担心基普。于是她拿起一本书，坐在外面晒太阳，但她无法思考书中的故事。大约十分钟后，天色暗了下来，开始下雨了。雨很大，好像天空裂开了一道口子似的。

“我下午要独自待在这个寒冷的谷仓里吗？”她心想，“现在下雨了，尼克肯定会回来吧？”

* * *

尼克已经滑水大约一个小时了，但天气变得如此糟糕，他再也无法在雨中看清东西了。

“我想我们最好停下来。”他的朋友大喊道，关掉小船的发动机，帮尼克爬上船。他们回到了沙滩上。

第47页

尼克脱去潜水衣时注意到一辆路虎车开了过来。车子停在他的车旁，一名男子跳了下来。尼克认出这个高个子男人就是他们来这儿的第一天晚上在酒馆遇到的那个人。他带着基普。

“你知道这只狗的主人在哪儿吗？”那人问。

“劳拉？你好，我是她的男朋友。”尼克说着伸出手与这位男士握手，“你好！我是尼克。”

“这是你们的狗，”兽医说，“也许你现在想让它回来？”

尼克大笑着说：“它不是我的狗！是劳拉的。”

“啊。嗯，她在哪儿？我需要把狗还给她。”兽医说。

“据我所知，她在上面的谷仓那里，”尼克说，“你能把狗带给她吗？我要换衣服，收拾我的东西。”

罗伯特决定不争辩了。他不喜欢这个人跟他说话的方式，但他并不感到惊讶。他以前遇到过像尼克这样的人。那些从伦敦来的人，他们表现得好像自己比其他人都重要。

罗伯特把他的路虎调头，再次出发去谷仓。今天下午他还有很多工作要做，他需要送还这只狗。一旦送走了基普，他就不必再与这两个讨厌的人有任何联系了。

第48页

他看了看基普。它是一只可爱的小狗，罗伯特有点儿舍不得把它送回去。

“我很遗憾你必须与那样的主人一起生活，”他一边开车前往谷仓，一边对基普说，“他们显然不知道该怎样好好地照看你。”

* * *

劳拉正在谷仓里烹饪黑莓。雨倾泻而下，这感觉非常好。她尽力忍着不去担心基普。然后她又听到了汽车引擎的声音。

她透过雨向窗外望去。这次不是跑车，而是一辆路虎——肯定是兽医，他终于来了。她走到门口。

兽医站在那儿，身上披着长雨衣，手里抱着基普。他把狗递给劳拉。

劳拉把基普抱进怀里，感觉对这只差一点儿失去的小狗有了一种新的爱。

“它还好吗？”劳拉问，“我一直很担心。”

“它很好……现在，”兽医说，“我希望你已经检查过谷仓是否还有毒药?”

第49页

“是的，我检查了。”劳拉说，感觉自己像一个小学生。

“我很忙，”兽医说，“我不需要不必要的急诊。”

“是的，我明白。”劳拉回答道。

“它是一只乡村狗，”兽医接着说，“你不能整天把它单独留在公寓里。”

劳拉看着兽医。为什么他听起来对她那么生气呢?他对她一无所知。

“我知道。”她说。她又看着他，但她突然觉得自己无法继续说下去了，即使她有很多话要讲。

她想告诉他，基普属于一位深爱它的老人，一位整天待在家里的老人。她想说的太多，但她没能说出来。她不知道是为什么。

“我应该付你多少钱?”她转而问道。

“请付一百英镑。”兽医答道。

她的心又开始狂跳。她没有一百英镑!至少她没有一百英镑来花在狗身上。

“我……我必须现在付吗?”她问，感觉从没这么蠢过。

第50页

兽医看了看她，有一阵子劳拉害怕他是真的生气了。然后正如头天晚上那样，他令她感到惊讶。

“没关系，”他说，“或许你路过时可以把钱送到诊所。”他转身离开。他留意到从厨房飘来的烹饪蓝莓的香味。这勾起了他不愿想起的回忆。

“我明天会把钱给你送去，”劳拉说，“我很抱歉……给你带来不便。”

劳拉又一次感觉想要多说些话。她想找机会解释一下。但就在这时，尼克开着跑车回来了。

“怎么回事?”他问道。

“我正在安排怎么给医生付钱，”劳拉说，“他救了基普的命。”

“他想要多少钱?”尼克问，仿佛兽医不在旁边。

“一百英镑，”劳拉说，“不过没关系。我明天进城回来后再付钱给他。”

“一百英镑！那只狗值那么多钱吗?”尼克问。

第51页

兽医愤怒地看着尼克。“如果你们一开始检查了谷仓是否有老鼠药，当然就不会在它身上花很多钱了。”兽医说。

“我们没有料到竟然会有老鼠药。什么样的地方会用老鼠药呢?”尼克问。

“人们不想有老鼠的地方。”兽医说。

“但是这太老土了，就像回到了一个世纪以前！”尼克说完大笑起来。兽医甚至没有微笑。

“瞧，”劳拉说，“我们犯了错。你说的对。我们以后会小心的。我明天要进城，届时我会去取钱。”知道在这种情况下最好礼貌一些，她又补充道：“谢谢你救了基普的命。如果没救活它的话，我不知道该怎么跟约瑟夫说。”

兽医转身离开时看了看劳拉，他想知道约瑟夫是谁。但他已经受够了这两个人，所以他没有问就开车走了。

第 8 章　悲惨的事故

第52页

劳拉和尼克坐在酒馆里吃着晚餐。

“你的狗真漂亮。”一个声音说道。

劳拉抬起头。和她说话的女士身材矮小，皮肤黝黑，有一双闪闪发光的蓝眼睛。

“哦，”那位女士接着说道，“它今天早上不是在兽医诊所里吗？”

“是的，”劳拉说，“你怎么知道的？”

“哦，我在那儿工作，”她说，“我叫玛吉，是兽医诊所的接待员。我喜欢动物，我一直喜爱动物。哦，看看它！”

“啊，”尼克说，“那么或许你能告诉我们为什么你的兽医那么粗鲁？”

“哦，他不是粗鲁，”玛吉说，“他只是伤心。如果你们知道两年前发生了什么事，你们就会明白的。从那之后，他几乎没有跟任何人说过话，特别是你们城里人。他没有时间陪你们。”

“那是为什么呢？”劳拉问。她意识到只是因为自己来自伦敦，罗伯特就没有给她解释的机会，这让她感到伤心。

第53页

“这个嘛……”玛吉开始讲。“你们介意吗？”她补充道，拉了一把椅子坐下。

“是这样的。罗伯特本打算娶基娅拉。她是意大利人，是一个可爱的女孩儿，漂亮、善良，而且聪明。她当时正参加培训成为一名医生。想象一下！一名兽医和一名医生！一天晚上，她决定去湖里游泳。那是初夏时节的一个美丽的傍晚，天还很亮。她和罗伯特下班后经常去游泳。但是那天晚上，罗伯特要工作到很晚，因此他告诉她自己晚些时候会到湖边跟她碰面，她就一个人先去了。湖区有些从伦敦来的男孩子，他们在湖边嬉闹，谈论玩摩托艇。周围还有很多人在湖边散步，享受着美好的夜晚。

“基娅拉下水后游了起来。他们说她沿着夕阳西下时在水面上形成的金色路线游着。如我刚才所说的，那是一个美丽的傍晚。”

玛吉停顿了一下，出神地抬头看了一小会儿天花板。然后她继续说起来。

“当她在那儿享受日落时，湖边的那些男孩子决定玩摩托艇。那时太阳落得很低了，或许是阳光晃眼……”

第54页

玛吉停下来喝了些饮料。很明显，她喜欢讲这个故事，而劳拉和尼克是很好的听众。

“……或者也许他们喝醉了，因为，不知怎么地，他们没有看到基娅拉。他们开得真的非常快，喊叫着，发出很大的噪声。突然……砰的一声。他们撞到了她。”

劳拉捂住了耳朵。她不想再听这个故事，但玛吉不愿停下来。

“他们说她直接飞到了空中。人们说，有好几秒钟，她看起来像一只大鸟，从水面上飞到空中，但当她落回水面后，她已经死了。”

玛吉抬头看了看劳拉和尼克。劳拉看起来很糟糕，她眼中含着泪水。尼克看起来很烦。

“水里到处都是血，那些骑摩托艇的男孩子们却消失不见了。他们第二天就走了，回伦敦去了，而从没有人抓住过他们。”

有几秒钟的沉默。

“这太惨了。”劳拉说。

“是的，更糟糕的是，罗伯特来到湖边，恰巧看到了基娅拉的死。他目睹了一切。他听见了摩托艇撞到她身体的声音，看到她飞到了空中。”

第55页

“从那以后，罗伯特就不再与城里人打交道了，而且他一直设法阻止人们在湖上玩摩托艇。他说摩托艇不仅危险，而且对乡村和野生生物不利。有人说他永远不会从基娅拉的死亡阴影中走出来，他会独自一人度过余生，但那只是在我没有得手的情况下了！”她说着笑了，“他真的很帅，你不这样认为吗？”她说这话的时候看着劳拉。劳拉感觉自己的脸红了。

* * *

周六早上，劳拉用小野营炉煮了咖啡，她把咖啡端给尼克。

“谢谢你，亲爱的。”尼克说着从她手中接过杯子。

“尼克。”劳拉说。她决定和他谈谈，她需要知道这个周末她到底能不能跟他待在一起。

“我们今天要做什么呢？我想也许我们可以一起去散散步。我觉得自从我们来到这儿我就没怎么看到过你。这里有一座漂亮的小山，我们可以从谷仓后面直接走上去。从山顶上一定能看到美景。”

第56页

“我来告诉你做什么，”尼克说，“你今天为什么不跟我一起去呢？我可以教你怎样玩摩托艇。”

劳拉看着他。他的眼睛闪闪发光，就像她第一次见到他时那样。当他第一次这样看着她时，她很容易就喜欢上了他。现在，出于某种她不明白的原因，这对她不起作用了。

“我不知道，”她说，“听了昨晚在酒馆里的那个女人告诉我们的那件事后，我想我不是很乐意去玩摩托艇了。”

“哦，你不要为这样的故事而担心，”尼克说，“这些当地人对游客非常生气。他们忘了实际上我们带来了很多钱。”

“但你不觉得她说得很有道理吗？”劳拉问。

“关于什么有道理？”尼克说。

“关于阻止玩摩托艇？”劳拉继续说。

“她没有建议阻止玩摩托艇。”尼克说。

“好吧，她自己没建议。她是在告诉我们兽医的想法。”劳拉说。

“是吗？我以为她只是在告诉我们，兽医不能从他女朋友死亡的阴影中走出来。他需要接受现实，继续生活。他不能指望仅仅因为一场意外每个人就放弃他们的运动。”尼克说。

第57页

“但关键是，他的女朋友被玩摩托艇的人害死了。难道你不认为这很可怕吗？”劳拉问。

“劳拉，如果我选择玩摩托艇，我就可以玩。如果那个男的对此有意见，他就应该住到别的地方或者闭嘴不谈此事。”尼克说。他下了床。

“我希望你跟我一起去，”他说，“你应该高兴的。我通常不会邀请女朋友和我一起玩摩托艇的。”

“对不起，尼克。我不能去，至少在听了那个故事后不能去。而且不管怎么说，我还得考虑基普。”

“基普！你想的全是那只狗。好吧，如果你不去，”尼克说，“我想立刻出门去湖上。我们只有两天的时间了。”

劳拉放弃了。“好吧。瞧，尼克，如果你又是出去一整个上午，我能用用你的车吗？我要带基普去散步，之后我需要去城里取些钱，我需要支付兽医的费用。”

“当然可以。开车到地方让我下车，车子你想用多久就用多久。”尼克答道。

第58页

半小时后，劳拉看着尼克喧闹地掠过湖面，他的摩托艇打破了清晨的宁静。她想起了玛吉昨晚给他们讲的故事。太可怕了！

“听过这样的故事后，尼克怎么还能径直去那儿呢？”劳拉一边开车离开，一边琢磨着，“我就是不明白他为什么想要像那样在湖上飞驰。对我而言，湖区的美就是它的安详静谧。为什么尼克不能理解这一点呢？”

第 9 章　再次独自一人

第59页

劳拉开车回到谷仓，找到基普。“咱们去走走吧，”她说，“我需要一些空气和运动。”

她开始向谷仓后面的山上走去。这是一个美丽的早晨，空气被昨天的雨水洗刷得很干净。很快她们就到了高处，俯视着下面的乡村。风景美极了。

“加油，基普！”劳拉喊道，“我们直接到山顶吧！”她们越爬越高，直到下面的湖泊看起来很小，而湖面上的摩托艇看似苍蝇。

她们爬到山顶后，劳拉找了一块石头坐在上面。她大口呼吸着清甜新鲜的空气，基普坐在她身旁。

“这对我来说太好了！”劳拉对基普说，“有时候我真的需要点儿空间，这让我头脑清醒。不知道我还能不能再住在像这样的地方。”

“我爱这些山、田野和树林。我想我的梦想就是在一个小镇上经营我的咖啡馆，住在像这样美丽的地方。伦敦很刺激，但那里太繁忙、太嘈杂。我不知道那里是否适合我。”她说着低头看着基普，“如果我住在像这样的地方，我甚至可能养一只像你一样的小狗。”

第60页

后来当她下山时，她才开始觉得奇怪，她没有把尼克纳入自己梦想的生活。

当她走到山脚下的路上时，她看到一辆路虎正向她这边驶来。基普在她的前面跑着。

劳拉的心怦怦直跳。是兽医！他是要告诉她不应该在路的这一边走吗？会斥责她让基普在田野里跑？会再次问她要钱？劳拉真希望自己可以找个地方躲起来，但为时已晚。那辆路虎正好停在她身边，罗伯特朝窗外看了看。

“它怎么样了？”他看着基普问道。

“它很好，好多了。”劳拉说。在他提到钱的事之前她赶紧说：“我今天晚些时候把钱给你送去。我要进城买点儿东西。我到了那里会取一些钱。”

“哦，好的。”罗伯特说。

一阵沉默，于是劳拉开始说话。她感到紧张。

第61页

“我想去看看当地的食品店。我想也许它们能帮上忙。我正在这个区域找供应商。我想在我的店里卖一些这附近的食物。”

“你的店？”他问。

“是一家带咖啡馆的食品店，”她发现自己在解释，“一家有机食品店。”

“哦。”他又说道。他吃惊地看着她。“其实，在科克茅斯有一家很好的有机食品店。我姑妈经营这家店。她的奶酪就是从这附近的农场买的。”

“真的吗？听起来不错。”劳拉说。

“稍后你带钱来时，我可以给你一些奶酪供应商的名字和地址。”他说。

“谢谢！”劳拉说着朝他一笑，但是他已经驾车离开了。

* * *

当天下午回到诊所，罗伯特从路虎车上跳下来。

玛吉正在门口等着。已经开始下雨了，她打着一把雨伞站着。罗伯特将身子探过她，用钥匙打开门。玛吉抬头看着他，希望他也能看看她，但是像往常一样罗伯特似乎没有注意到她。

第62页

“今天下午我们都有什么预约？”她开启电脑时，他问道。

她读着给自己的动物预约的人的名单。稍后巡诊时，他需要去看一只羊，还有一匹小马。但是现在有一个女人要抱来一只不吃东西的兔子，还有一个人要带来一只大狗。

“哦，”玛吉说，“我忘了告诉你了，那个女人——那个养了一只名叫基普的可爱小狗的女人——她昨天上午打来电话并留了言。她想知道你为什么还没有把狗带回去。她听起来很担心。”

罗伯特看着玛吉。“你昨天为什么不告诉我？”他说。

“我觉得不重要啊，”她回答道，“反正我知道你已经去那儿了。”

罗伯特什么也没说，就进了他的诊室。

那天下午晚些时候，他正和一个带着猫的女孩儿道别时，玛吉就在诊室门口探头进来。她递给罗伯特一杯茶。

“那位叫劳拉的女士来了，”玛吉说，“她还带着那只漂亮的小狗。她已经付了钱，但是她说你有东西要给她，一个农民的地址还是什么的。”

第63页

罗伯特放下茶。“是的，我知道她要什么，”他对玛吉说，“让她进来。”

劳拉走进房间。她一只手抱着基普，有那么一秒罗伯特感觉自己的心跳加快了，这种感觉他几乎都忘记了。这与那只小狗有关，他心想。也许他只是希望抱着狗的是他而不是劳拉。

“那么它现在没事了吧？没再有什么问题吧？”罗伯特把手放在基普的头上问道。他的手不小心碰到了劳拉的手臂，她快速躲开了。

“它很好。谢谢。”劳拉说。她感到很惊讶，兽医又问了她这个问题。今天上午他已经问过她基普是否好了。

她看着兽医。他正充满爱意地看着基普，劳拉心想。然后她想道：“不，这太疯狂了。兽医经常给狗看病，他怎么会喜欢基普胜过他照顾的其他狗呢？”

玛吉打断了他们。“皮尔斯夫人带着她的拉布拉多犬想见你，”她对罗伯特说，“它最近表现很差，她希望带它看心理医生。”

“好。告诉她我一会儿就去见她。”罗伯特说，玛吉离开了房间。

第64页

一想到给狗看病的心理医生，劳拉就努力忍住没笑出来，她想知道罗伯特是否也在忍住不笑。

第65页

他看了看劳拉，有那么一秒钟他们的眼神相遇了，然后他又移开了视线。

“这听起来很可笑，”他一边说一边在纸上抄下一个地址，“但我有这种想法，人们经常带着他们的动物来找我，不是因为动物生病了，而是因为他们自己需要一些帮助。”

“真的吗？那真有趣。”劳拉说，兽医突然这样对她说话，她感到很惊讶。

“是的。这只表现不好的狗……其实是它的主人病了。她患有严重的抑郁症。是她需要心理医生，而不是狗。或者也许，”他补充道，“狗需要心理医生，是因为它的主人需要心理医生。”

这是她听到他说的最长的句子，劳拉很吃惊——对他说的话既吃惊又很感兴趣。

“那你会告诉主人去看医生吗？我的意思是，当你知道他们病了的时候。”她问他。

“那不是我的工作，”罗伯特说，“我可以倾听，但至于告诉他们要做什么就不是我的工作了。”

“我有时候感觉在我的咖啡馆里也是这样，”劳拉说，“人们告诉我各种各样的事，但我不能告诉他们该做什么。有时，人们只是需要说说话。”

第66页

“完全正确。”罗伯特说，“好了，这些是你想要的地址。”

“谢谢，”劳拉说，“我得走了，好让你继续工作。”

劳拉离开诊所时感觉有点儿奇怪。兽医说的话比他以往说的都要多。他和她说话时，好像知道她会明白他在说什么。

“既然我已经付了钱，我就不会再看到他了。”她心想。

当她驱车离开时，她意识到这最后一个想法使她感到悲伤。

“那是因为我想让他知道，我不是他所认为的无可救药的伦敦人。”她心想，试图解释自己的感受。

第 10 章　新生命

第67页

劳拉看了看兽医给她写在纸上的地址，拿出一张地图。离谷仓很近的地方有一个制作和销售奶酪的农场。是的，她可以开车回谷仓，然后带着基普走着去农场。

半小时后，劳拉向农场走去，基普跟在她的旁边。农场几乎就在山顶上，穿过田野、走上山很不容易。天空再次乌云密布，要下雨了。

劳拉把基普夹在一只胳膊下，走向农舍的门，她敲了敲门。一些母鸡正在农场的院子里跑来跑去。

没有人来开门。从院子的另一边传来母牛的叫声，声音很大，听起来好像挺痛苦的。基普叫了起来。

劳拉又敲了敲门，然后放弃了，她穿过院子朝奶牛发出叫声的地方走去。绕过一个谷仓，她看到一头奶牛侧躺着，一个年轻人在它上方弯着腰。那人看了看她。

第68页

“它要下崽了，”他喊道，“但小牛犊被卡住了。我已经给兽医打过电话了。我以为你是他呢。”

劳拉不知所措。“我碍事了，”她说，“我本想问问你的奶酪，那我下次再来吧。”

“其实，你可以帮上忙，”那人说，“等到兽医来了就行。如果你能把这只狗拴起来，让牛的头别动。”

“哦，天哪，”劳拉心想，“这是我最没有料到的事。”她把基普的链子拴到大门上，然后回到那个农民身边。

“按住它的头不要动，跟它说说话，”农民说，“我必须用绳子拴住小牛犊的腿。是臀位。”

劳拉知道臀位意味着小牛出生的方向反了。

“这对于小牛和母牛来说都会很危险。”农民说。

母牛痛苦地大声哞哞叫着。劳拉温柔地摸着它的鼻子。“没事的，”她说，“会没事的。”

“我这头需要帮忙，”农民大喊道，“我们需要迅速把小牛弄出来。”

第69页

劳拉开始感到害怕，她以前从未做过这样的事。她绕到奶牛的尾巴处，帮农民拉绳子。

“它就要出来了。”他说。

奶牛又大叫了一声，农民往外拉绳子，他的脸被汗水浸湿了。奶牛再次大声哞哞叫起来。

“不行，它被卡住了。我们得马上放弃。我只是期望兽医能快点儿来。”

又一次提及兽医，劳拉的心怦怦直跳。或者这只是努力帮助小牛出来的缘故？

“让我们再试一次。”农民说。劳拉尽最大努力拉绳子。

又过了几分钟，小牛终于生出来了。农民抱着它直到它叫了一声，然后才把它放到地上。它抖了抖身子。奶牛转身碰了它一下，短短几分钟后小牛就靠着纤细的腿站了起来。

劳拉看着小牛。“太神奇了！”她说，“看着动物出生是一件很神奇的事情！”

“是的。谢天谢地！”农民说，“我以为我们会失去它们两个，还好我们及时。”

第70页

他转向她说：“你没有料到这种事，是吧？你是来询问……什么来着？”

“奶酪的事。我……我希望你能让我品尝一下你的奶酪。我在伦敦有一家商店，我正在找新的供应商。但也许这时候问此事不合适。”劳拉解开了基普，又把它抱了起来。

“不，没关系。奶酪……嗯。你最好进屋里来，如果你不介意等我洗洗手的话。”

劳拉坐在农舍的厨房里。农民洗好手后拿了一些奶酪给她品尝。

“这些奶酪味道好极了。真的很特别，”劳拉说，“我真的想订购一些。”

“太棒了！”农民说，他取来纸，写下自己的电子邮箱地址。

“哦，天哪，都这个点了，”劳拉突然说道，“我得去湖边接尼克。”

“尼克？”农民问。

“是的。他是我的男朋友，他在玩摩托艇，”劳拉解释道，“我答应六点到那儿接他，这样我们就能够早点儿到酒馆吃饭。”

第71页

她跟农民说好一回到伦敦就给他发电子邮件，然后就离开了，她穿过田野，基普在旁边跟着跑。她对自己感到满意。这个下午竟然如此令人兴奋，她还找到了一些好吃的奶酪可以卖。

她刚刚消失在树林中，罗伯特的路虎车就开到了农场。

“你来得太晚了，”农民边说边从房子里走出来，“小牛出生了。我觉得它没什么问题。”

“无论如何我要给它检查一下。”罗伯特说。他很了解这个农民，他的每一头奶牛对他而言都是特别的。

“我很抱歉花了这么长时间才来。山顶农场也有个急诊。有一匹马的腿断了。”

“别担心——我很幸运，有一位女士来得正是时候，”农民说，“她帮了我。”

“哦？”罗伯特说。

“是的。她在伦敦开了一家店，她来找我要奶酪，结果却帮了我的忙。对她来说真是一次历险。”

“哦，那很好，”罗伯特说，意识到农民说的一定是劳拉，“那她现在在哪儿呢？”

第72页

“她走了，去湖边接她的男朋友，这样他们就能早点儿去白牛酒馆。他们显然是游客。”

“是的，”罗伯特说，“我想我见过他们。”

“最差劲的一类，”农民说，“玩摩托艇的人。”

“嗯，男的是，女的似乎不感兴趣。”罗伯特说。农民做了个鬼脸，罗伯特没再说什么。

检查完母牛和小牛犊之后，罗伯特开车回到诊所，玛吉正在那儿整理东西。

“谢天谢地，到星期六晚上了。我不用随叫随到了。”他说。

看见他笑了，玛吉说：“今晚去白牛酒馆喝一杯怎么样？”

“哦，好。”罗伯特回答。玛吉看着他，无法相信自己的好运。

“你刚才答应了是吗？”她问道。

“是的，我刚才答应了。”罗伯特说。玛吉大笑个不停。

第 11 章　酒馆邂逅

第73页

劳拉开车回到湖边，她坐在车里。尼克还在水上玩，大雨开始下了起来。基普坐在她旁边。她和基普看着雨落下，湖上的摩托艇在水面上跳跃。

尼克终于回来了。他把潜水服扔进车里。

“我们直接去酒馆吧。我准备好吃饭了。”他说。

她渐渐习惯了尼克的做派。他没打算问她更喜欢做什么。他做了所有的决定，并期待她同意。他们开车时沉默地坐着。

过了几分钟，劳拉感到这样的沉默很不舒服。

“看来你今天过得不错啊？”她问他。

“很棒！你呢？”他回答。

“是的。我去为我的商店找奶酪供应商，结果帮了一头母牛生产！”

“不错。”尼克说。

第74页

"不错?"劳拉开始生气了。尼克都没有好好听她说话吗?

"不，尼克，不只是不错——是棒极了！亲眼看见——帮助一个新生命出生。没有比这更好的了。这让我觉得我的生活很乏味。"

"什么？比一头牛的生活乏味?"尼克大笑。

"不，我的意思是比兽医的生活乏味。"劳拉说。

"兽医的生活?"尼克问。

"是的。我的意思是，给动物接生——这是兽医的工作。这个工作那么重要，那么有趣，那么感人。"劳拉说。

"兽医也在那儿吗?"尼克问。

"没有，只有我和那个农民。"劳拉说。

"这么说兽医不太称职，对吧？别人需要他时，他甚至没有出现。现在，"尼克说着牵起她的手，微笑地看着她，"今晚我们吃什么?"

* * *

今天晚上酒馆里热闹了一些。

"你要吃什么?"尼克问劳拉。

她看了一会儿菜单，觉得很难做决定。她的脑海里还想着其他的事，使她感到既不开心又很困惑。

第75页

最后她说："我要肉和蔬菜饼。你呢?"

"炸鱼加薯条，"他说，"我受够了这些本地食物。"

"我去点吧，"劳拉说，"同时我再点些喝的。"劳拉说完走向吧台。

* * *

玛吉和罗伯特正坐在吧台旁的凳子上。

"今天下午来的那只波斯猫很漂亮是吧?"玛吉问，"它有一双最神奇的眼睛!"

罗伯特笑了，但什么也没说。玛吉很甜美。可是为什么她只想谈论动物——而且通常是那些他最不感兴趣的动物?

"知道吗，你还不如养只猫呢，"玛吉继续说，"有它们在身边很好，而且它们能照顾自己。"

"瞧，玛吉，我知道你是好意，但是我现在对养猫真的不感兴趣。"罗伯特说。

玛吉做了个鬼脸，假装受伤。"对不起，"她说，"只是，你要知道，我担心你一个人生活。"

"别担心，"罗伯特说，"你可能很难理解，玛吉，但有些人喜欢独居胜过跟任何人生活在同一个屋檐下——不管是和长着两条腿的还是和长着四条腿的。"

第76页

"但你是个兽医!"玛吉说。

"这并不意味着我想和猫生活在一起。动物有它们的地位，是的，"罗伯特解释道，"正如你所知道的，我喜欢帮助它们。我尤其喜欢帮助农民，所以今天下午我感觉真是糟透了，我错过了帮助那头小牛出生。"

"啊!"玛吉说着做了个鬼脸。

"你'啊'是什么意思?"罗伯特问。

"我不知道——一想到，你知道，把牛犊从奶牛的身体里拽出来。"玛吉说。

"帮助动物接生实际上是我工作中最精彩的部分，"罗伯特说，"这比给猫喂药治疗感冒更令人兴奋。目睹一个动物出生是很美好的。”

“什么东西这么美好啊？”一位年长的妇人从吧台对面走过来与他们交谈。她头发灰白，穿着时髦的丝绸上衣和裙子。

“芭芭拉！”罗伯特说着站起来亲吻她。“非常高兴见到你。你在这里做什么？”

“我在吃饭。”她说着向吧台另一边的一张桌子旁的男子点了点头，“伊恩邀请我的。”

第77页

“太好了！”罗伯特说，“玛吉，这是我姑妈，芭芭拉。她在科克茅斯经营一家食品店。芭芭拉，这是我的接待员，玛吉。”

“你好，玛吉！”芭芭拉说。

她看着罗伯特和他的接待员，心想：“看来罗伯特终于又开始进行社交了。看起来他好像交了一个女朋友。”

“我们忙了一天，”罗伯特开始解释，“玛吉提议喝一杯，然后……”他停住了。他能感觉到有一个热乎乎的东西贴着自己的腿。他低头一看，只见两只棕色的眼睛正抬头看着他。

“基普！”他欢快地说。

“我很抱歉。”劳拉正匆匆朝他们走来。“它看到了你，就朝你跑来了，”劳拉对罗伯特说，“我没能拦住它。它显然已经非常喜欢你了。”

罗伯特微笑着看着狗，又抬头看了看劳拉。

“没关系，”他说，“听着，你在这里正好。这是我姑妈芭芭拉。她在科克茅斯经营食品店，我今天上午跟你说过的。芭芭拉，这是劳拉。”

“哦！”劳拉说，“很高兴见到您。我也经营一家食品店，但是在伦敦。”

第78页

芭芭拉看了看劳拉，然后看了看罗伯特。

“那么……你们是怎么认识的?”她问。她知道罗伯特不喜欢伦敦人，他对劳拉这么友好似乎很奇怪。

第79页

“哦，罗伯特救了基普的命。”劳拉说着指了指她的小狗。

“你今天下午帮一头母牛接生了。”罗伯特突然说。劳拉看着他。

“是的，”她说，“我……我只是碰巧在那儿……而且，嗯，你不在……”

“你抢了我的工作。”罗伯特面无笑容地说。

劳拉看着他，又感到害怕起来。他真的生她的气了吗？

然后他笑了。“别看起来那么担心，”他说，“我是开玩笑的。”

“不，但是他说的对！”玛吉直视着劳拉说，“如果你一点儿都不了解动物，帮助它们是很危险的。小牛可能会死。”

“哦！”劳拉说，“但它没死。不管怎么说，我不是有意要帮忙。是那个农民让我帮忙的。那儿没有其他人。他在等……等……”

“他在等我，”罗伯特对玛吉说，“但我当时在处理那匹马，那匹断了腿的马。”

“好了，我现在必须回到伊恩那儿了。如果你想来我的商店看看，我很乐意和你多聊聊。”芭芭拉对劳拉说，“我明天上午在，但十二点关门。我们总是在周日下午花很长时间好好散散步。”

第80页

“好的，我愿意去，”劳拉说，“谢谢您。很高兴见到您。”

劳拉走回尼克身边时，她能感觉到玛吉的眼睛一直在注视着她。

第 12 章　新朋友

第81页

劳拉回到了尼克身边，而基普则待在罗伯特的脚边。她尽量不去想罗伯特和玛吉那么惬意地坐在一起，也不去想玛吉看她的眼神。她感觉到了什么，但没有去想到底是什么。好消息是她为自己的店找到了一些新的供应商，现在她打算明天去拜访那位友善的芭芭拉女士。她们可以彼此交流交流想法。

"哇！"劳拉坐下来时尼克说，"那不是昨晚和我们谈话的那个女人吗？"

"是啊，"劳拉说，"怎么啦？"

"嗯，她很可爱。我不明白她为什么会和那个讨厌的兽医在一起。"

劳拉注视着吧台旁的那两个人，她之前从来没有认真看过玛吉。

"我觉得她非常漂亮，"劳拉说，"但兽医长得也好看，而且他真的相当友善。他们俩很般配。"

她盯着吧台对面的那两个人。他们聊天时低着头，她不知道他们在聊什么。

第82页

* * *

第二天早上劳拉醒来时，尼克已经出门了。厨房里有一张便条，上面写着："去湖上了。午餐时回来。"

劳拉感到不高兴，但她对此无能为力。她坐下来，看着基普。

"发生了什么，基普？"她问小狗，"尼克跟我当初想的不一样。

我猜我也不是他当初想的那种人。总是这样子！我是怎么搞的？我怎么总是选错人呢？”

她又想起了他们到这儿的第一个晚上。她是如何不得不穿过夜色独自开车去找兽医的。看起来，尼克不想做什么事的时候，他就是不去做。他对这里的乡村的看法也让她不高兴，不管她怎么努力去理解。

“他并不是真的想让我在这儿，”她想，“我开始觉得他不适合我。”

突然，劳拉想起来芭芭拉邀请她今天上午去看她的商店，她一下子感到心情愉悦一些了。

她心想：“我有我自己的生活要过。总之，谁需要男人啊，对吧，基普？”

第83页

她看了看手表。现在是十点一刻。开车大概半个小时能到科克茅斯。如果她现在出发，到那儿时间绰绰有余。

幸运的是，尼克把车留给了她，她上了车，出发前往科克茅斯。

这是一个美丽的早晨。昨天的雨让万物像玻璃一样在晨光中闪耀，色彩鲜艳。仔细思考过她与尼克的关系后，她感觉头脑清醒了。

“我打算努力工作，”她想，“从芭芭拉那儿尽可能多学点儿东西。眼下我不打算去操心感情的事了。”

芭芭拉的商店在商业街的一端。劳拉停车后和基普沿街走着。这是一个有趣的小镇，有一些不错的商店。

劳拉找到芭芭拉的店，走了进去。

芭芭拉从商店的后面走出来，热情地微笑着。

“你好，亲爱的。你能来真是太好了。”她说。

第84页

“贾妮在替我照看商店，所以我们可以聊聊。到后面来吧。”

劳拉跟着她，注意到那一罐罐待售的有趣的食物。

“那么，”几分钟后芭芭拉说，“跟我说说你的商店吧，你怎么开始的、卖什么东西，等等。”

这家商店是一栋大房子的门面，现在她们坐在厨房里。芭芭拉给了劳拉一杯自制的柠檬水。

劳拉给芭芭拉讲了她在伦敦的商店的所有情况，她们聊了很久，没有留意到时间。

“你必须品尝一下这些馅饼，”芭芭拉边说边从烤箱里拿出一些东西，“本地的一位女士为我做的。它们会在你的咖啡馆里卖得很好的。罗伯特喜欢这个。”她递给劳拉一块看起来很美味的馅饼。

“罗伯特？”劳拉咬着馅饼问道。

“是的。他喜欢我的食物，”芭芭拉说，“你觉得他怎么样？他可能看起来有点儿不友好，可是他心肠好。你知道他为什么这么少言寡语吗？”

“我听说了他女朋友的悲剧。”劳拉说。

第85页

“是的。这件事糟透了，”芭芭拉说，“对他影响很深。”

“是的。”劳拉说。

“不仅仅是因为她的死，”芭芭拉说，“而是因为没有人抓到害死她的人。罗伯特认为，虽然人们仍被允许在湖上玩摩托艇，但可能会发生另一起事故。”

“嗯，他想的有道理。”劳拉说。

“但是他需要向前看，”芭芭拉说，“停留在这样的凄惨记忆中而不能自拔不是一件好事。他需要忘记发生的事，重新开始充实的生活。”

“这对他来说一定很难。”劳拉说着想起了玛吉之前在酒馆里的悲惨描述，“不管怎样，他最近不是在跟他的接待员约会吗？”

“嗯，他昨晚是和她在一起，”芭芭拉说，“但依我看，她不是他喜欢的类型。（她继续说）好了，你觉得这些馅饼怎么样？”

“非常完美！”劳拉说，慢慢领会这位女士给她讲的所有内容，“您说罗伯特也喜欢它们？”

“哦，他喜欢所有好吃的食物，”芭芭拉说，“或者说至少他过去喜欢。基娅拉死之前，他自己很会做饭。她死后，他就对一切失去了兴趣。一切，除了他的工作。他真的很关心农民和他们的动物。他是一个好人，他真的是。”

第86页

“是的。我非常感谢他，因为两件事：把我介绍给您，还救了基普的命。”劳拉摸了摸基普的头。

“它是一只漂亮的小狗。你一定很喜欢它。”芭芭拉说。

“哦，它不是我的，”劳拉回答，“我是替我隔壁的一位老人照看它——我们来湖区的前一天，他不得不住进医院。我自己真的不想养狗，尤其是在伦敦，在那里它们不怎么运动。不过有趣的是，当你整天和它们待在一起时，你就会对它们产生依恋。”

“是的，我相信你会。”芭芭拉说。她把身体向后靠着，笑着对劳拉说：“那么，你享受在湖区的假期吗？”

“哦，是的，我喜欢这里，”劳拉感慨地说，“我一直很喜欢这里，我小时候来过。我原以为也许这里已经变了，但景色依旧美丽。”

“这里比以前更热闹了。湖上做水上运动的人熙熙攘攘的。”

第87页

“是的，这点改变了。我是和我的男朋友尼克来的。他喜欢玩摩托艇，但我不感兴趣。我更喜欢散步。所以一直是我自己和基普一起出去走走。”

“哦，听着！今天下午你为什么不和我们一起去呢？我告诉过你我们每个星期天午饭后都会去散步。你想加入我们吗？好多人会来，非常欢迎你来。”

“哦，我非常愿意。”劳拉说。

“我们下午两点在科尼斯顿湖见面。期待稍后能见到你。”

第 13 章　散步

第88页

“你没告诉我你要去哪儿就走了！”劳拉回到谷仓时，尼克生气地说。

“我很抱歉，尼克。你没等我就走了，我忘了告诉你，我必须在十二点前赶到科克茅斯。”

“好吧。嗯，我想回去做水上运动，所以咱们走吧！”

“我们还没吃午饭呢。”劳拉说。

“等你的时候我吃了个三明治，”尼克说，“真的，劳拉，我不想再浪费任何时间了。我们明天就要走了。”

“尼克，你满脑子想的似乎都是你的水上运动！我不得不说，我发现这很难接受。”

尼克抱着一堆潜水服，在走向跑车的途中停了下来，回头看着劳拉。

“是吗？你知道这就是我来湖区的目的呀。这就是我通常一个人来的原因。我邀请你来是因为我原以为你是那种会理解我的女人。”

第89页

“在某种程度上我的确理解。但是尼克，我们几乎没有任何时间在一起。”劳拉说。

“那是因为你对摩托艇不感兴趣。”尼克回答。

“不，我不是……”劳拉开始说。

“还因为你带来了那只笨狗！”尼克接着说。

“尼克，不是这样的。”劳拉说。

“第一天你就花了一晚上的时间开车到乡村寻找那个坏脾气的兽医。”尼克说。

“就一个晚上！而且尼克，我别无选择，我是为了约瑟夫才那么做的。”劳拉说。

“没错。你把一个老头看得比我重要。”尼克说。

“尼克，狗差点儿死了！但从那以后，我们在这里待了三天，我们也没花时间待在一起。你总是在湖上玩！”劳拉说。

“那你为什么不和我一起去呢？或许你会喜欢。”尼克说。

“不，我不会喜欢的。因为我在乎当地人的想法，而你不在乎。”劳拉说。

“对，劳拉，我不在乎！如果你认为我会停止做自己最喜欢的事，那你就错了！我每周工作七天，每天工作二十四小时，就是为了赚足够的钱来生活，而玩水上摩托艇是我最大的兴趣。”尼克说。

第90页

“我只是不能相信，你对一个女人的死毫不在乎。”劳拉说。

“对，她死了。她的死不是我的错。人们玩摩托艇的时候她还游泳！这就是她为什么会死。如果说是谁的过错的话，那也是她自己的错！”尼克说。

“摩托艇太糟糕了，对于……”劳拉说。

尼克生气地上了车，发动了引擎。劳拉跑到汽车旁。

“对不起，尼克，”她说，“我不应该说这些话。我控制不了。有时我对事情的感受很强烈，我不能只把它们憋在心里。”尼克没有回答。劳拉上车坐在他的旁边。“听我说，尼克，如果你又要去玩摩托艇，今天下午可以把车给我用吗？有人邀请我去散步，我真的想去。”

“散步？和谁？”尼克问道。

“和一位女士——昨天晚上我在酒馆里遇到的那位。她在科克茅斯开店。”

“哦，好吧。你可以用车。”尼克说，没有看她。

第91页

* * *

那天下午，劳拉回去见芭芭拉和她的朋友们。她期待着和熟悉湖区的人一起散步。

她开车时意识到自己很难过。和尼克在一起不合适，她已经知道他们回到伦敦后会发生什么。一旦他们回到自己的生活中，一切都会结束。劳拉想起了自己的公寓和工作。是的，这些让她忙碌。但若没人分享，它们又显得多么空虚、多么没有意义。找到一个真正了解自己的生活追求的人真是太难了。

她看了看基普。“难怪有人选择狗做朋友，”她大声说，“你就简单多了。”

她到达了芭芭拉告诉她的会面地点，站在那里感觉有点儿害羞。那里有几位老人，他们穿着步行靴，拿着手杖。突然基普跳了起来，开心地叫着。

劳拉抬头望去。从村庄穿过田野走来的是罗伯特。劳拉感到很惊讶。罗伯特来到人群中，默默地站在他们中间。

第92页

芭芭拉走到劳拉身边，贴着她的耳朵悄悄说起来。“我劝罗伯特来的，”她说，“这么多年来这是他第一次同意跟一群人一起散步。我们应该高兴。”

他们开始沿着山脚下走。基普想去找罗伯特，最后劳拉让它带着她去了他身边。

“嗨。”她说。

“芭芭拉邀请我来散步的。”他低着头说，好像很尴尬，“通常我不喜欢跟一群人散步，我更喜欢一个人。可是她要我来，我妥协了。”

他们此刻在一条小溪边走着，空气清新而干净。

很快他们开始爬山，乡村在他们身后渐渐远去。罗伯特走在前面，基普紧跟着他。于是劳拉开始和芭芭拉并排走，她们一起轻松地聊着各自的商店。

“我刚才一直在听劳拉说她的商店和咖啡馆，”后来当他们都停下来休息时，芭芭拉告诉罗伯特，“听起来很不错。我们一致认为我的馅饼在那里会卖得很好。”

“很好。这很棒。”罗伯特说。

基普又朝罗伯特跑过来。“她的狗似乎很喜欢你，罗伯特，”芭芭拉说，“嗯，狗不是她的，当然，但是……”

第93页

“你是什么意思？”罗伯特问。

“哦，她没跟你说吗？这只狗是一个老人的，但是就在她出发来这里前他住院了。她是在替他照看狗。”

“哦！”罗伯特说，突然感觉一切都理清了。“哦，现在我明白了。”

他望着人群对面的劳拉。她确实与自己起初想的大不相同。这么说狗不是她的。她不是自己之前认为的那种养狗只为赶时髦的可恶的城里人。“可是她怎么会和那个讨厌的男人约会呢？”他心想。

他们继续往山上爬。芭芭拉转过身来等一个朋友，于是罗伯特和劳拉发现他俩肩并肩地走着。

罗伯特朝芭芭拉在等的那位女士点头示意了一下。“她是费洛斯夫人，”罗伯特说，“有一天晚上她给我打电话，因为她的猫打喷嚏了。猫没问题，不过她却讲了大半个晚上。你明白我的意思吗？”

“你的意思是，她才是那个需要你的人，不是猫？”

第94页

“对。”罗伯特答道。

“你觉得每个带动物来找你看病的人都是他们自己有问题吗？”劳拉问。

“不是每个人，不是。”罗伯特回答道。

他斜着眼看着她，劳拉终于感觉到他正对自己热情起来。

“我呢？”劳拉突然问，“那天晚上我来找你——你觉得是我需要帮助而不是基普吗？”

“啊，”罗伯特说，他突然笑了，“嗯，基普确实需要帮助。它吃了一些对它不好的东西。但或许你正在做对你自己不好的事！我认为这很可能是真的。”

“比如什么？”劳拉笑着问道。她喜欢这种游戏。这让她想起了她在店里与乔一起玩的游戏，猜测人和他们的职业。

“只有你知道。”罗伯特说。然后，他给基普扔了一根树枝，开始追着它跑，留下劳拉疑惑不解：“他是什么意思呢？”

第 14 章　罗伯特的房子

第95页

两个小时后，他们回到了山脚下。

“这次散步很愉快，”劳拉对芭芭拉说，“非常感谢您邀请我。我很开心，基普也是。可是我现在得走了。我们明天要离开了，我得收拾行李。”

“好吧，别忘了给我打电话或发电子邮件，告诉我你在店里的订单，”芭芭拉说，“或者其他任何你可能想要的东西。很高兴认识你。罗伯特，(她说着转向兽医) 你不是说你把路虎车留在汽车修理厂了，需要搭车回家吗？”

“是的。”罗伯特说。

“劳拉，你住在罗伯特去的方向，是吗？你不介意捎他一程，对吧？”芭芭拉问。

劳拉担心自己要脸红了。她不知道为什么。

“没问题。”她说，让头发吹散在脸上。

第96页

“谢谢。”他说。

“还有，”芭芭拉看着劳拉说，“我会在十一月中旬前把第一批订单发给你。”

“如果您不介意，那就太好了。正好能赶上圣诞节。”劳拉看着芭芭拉的眼睛，觉得自己好像交了一个朋友。那为什么她也觉得这位女士在欺骗她呢？

在跑车里罗伯特坐在劳拉身旁。在这辆小小的车里他似乎太高，不适合坐在乘客座位上。

“这太奇怪了，”劳拉心想，“真奇怪，他突然出现在我身边，在尼克的车里，当初我以为……以为……当初我怎么想的？我以为他讨厌我呢！我以为他没时间跟城里人相处呢！”然后她想起了他在山上说过的话。

“你说也许我在做一些对自己不好的事情是什么意思？”她问。

“啊，”罗伯特说，“只有你知道问题的答案。”

当劳拉开到一条小路上时，他们沉默了几分钟。然后罗伯特说：“好了，我的房子就在这条路的前面。非常感谢你送我一程。”

第97页

“不用谢。”他下车时劳拉说。

他背对着劳拉站了一会儿，仿佛在决定要做什么——走进他的房子还是转身。

然后他突然转向她说：“我不知道你……你想要喝杯茶吗？”

劳拉看了下手表。尼克可能至少还要在湖上待半个小时。她可以花几分钟的时间和兽医一起喝杯茶。她很高兴他邀请了她。根据玛吉所说的，他通常并不很善于交际。或许现在他和玛吉变得亲密了，他正在学着跟别人在一起时变得放松。也许玛吉最终帮他走出了基娅拉死亡的阴影。

基普愉快地叫着，看着罗伯特，张着嘴，仿佛在微笑。

“我觉得基普已经替我做了决定！”她说。

罗伯特的房子又大又旧，不过出奇地温暖和明亮。他把她领进一间有落地窗的大客厅，窗外是美丽的山景。

他走过一扇门消失了，进了一个一定是厨房的地方，基普跟在他后面，看上去就像在家里般自在。

第98页

“嘿，基普，到这里来。”劳拉一边说，一边跟着小狗，但是基普已经躺在了罗伯特的脚边。

“它记得。”罗伯特说完笑了。劳拉之前没怎么看他笑过。他的嘴宽宽的，使他的脸发亮，仿佛太阳刚出来。

“你知道，我要再次感谢你救了基普的命。”劳拉抬头看着罗伯特，害羞地说。

他正在把牛奶倒进两杯茶里。“这只是我的工作。”他说。

“是的，但如果它死了，我不知道该怎么对约瑟夫说。我感觉糟透了。我不习惯养狗。我没想到要检查谷仓。”即使是现在，她仍对罗伯特感到紧张，而她紧张时就会不停地说话。

“约瑟夫是一个很要好的朋友吗？”他问。

“是的。他是一位可爱的老人，在伦敦住在我隔壁。我们来这儿的前一晚他生病了。他让我替他照看基普。他说他害怕基普会比他先死。我觉得他是害怕如果基普死了，他就没有活下去的理由了。他孤身一人，只有他的狗。”

第99页

“我们去那里面坐吧。”罗伯特说，他们回到漂亮的客厅。外面，雨幕掠过山丘和树林。

“那如果基普死了，那个老人就没有活下去的理由了，”他重复道，“我知道那种感觉……”

劳拉等着，她意识到罗伯特要告诉她基娅拉的事，要说他自己的事。她不想说话，不想打破沉默，等着他说话。

他站在窗边，望着外面的乡村。她看着他那手工编织的套头衫下宽阔的肩膀，裹在旧的灯芯绒裤子里的大长腿，还有他那看似没有梳理过的金黄色头发。突然，她明确地知道为什么他让她感到很紧张了，因为她发现他是如此有魅力。

她希望自己没有发现这种感觉，希望自己从没见过他，希望这个周末没来湖区。因为有一件事是肯定的，这个男人绝不会那样看她。他现在与玛吉在一起。还有，虽然和尼克发展得不顺利，但她仍然与他在一起。

“我之前完全误会你了，”罗伯特突然转身看着她说，“我欠你一个道歉。”

第100页

“不，不，没关系。”劳拉说。

“我对你粗鲁、不友善。我以为那天上午是你出门玩摩托艇了。我以为这是你的狗，你不知道如何妥善地照看它。我还以为……我以为你养狗只是为了赶时髦。但我错了。我希望你接受我的道歉。”他说。

“我当然接受你的道歉。”劳拉说。

“我的意思是……我想说的是，事实上你和我之前想的完全相反。你很体贴，又这么善良，周末出门还为一位老人照看这只小狗。我的问题是……我的问题是，自从我的女朋友去世后，我发现很难去……去……相信任何人……她遇害后有很长时间我真的觉得自己没有了活下去的理由。”

“那当然很正常。任何人都会是这种感觉 。”劳拉说。

“然后我活下去的理由变成阻止人们玩摩托艇。除了工作，那是我唯一关心的，”罗伯特继续说，“我恨与之有关系的每一个人。像那样恨别人是很不好的。”

第101页

“你控制不了。这可以理解。在这些美丽的湖泊上看到摩托艇是挺糟糕的。它们看起来很可怕，声音听起来挺讨厌！”劳拉说。

“我一直想不再恨别人。我想再次感受美好的东西。我希望感受……”

“什么？”劳拉轻轻地问。

“嗯，我想说的是，我想我又开始……对某个人……有了感觉。”罗伯特说。

劳拉突然觉得喘不过气来。她担心自己会完全窒息。她不希望他告诉自己他对玛吉的感觉。她就是不想听，不是现在她自己开始对这个男人有感觉时。

“我必须走了。”她说着站起来，放下茶杯，“我要去水上运动中心接尼克。走吧，基普！”

第 15 章　两次道别

第102页

劳拉想尽快离开这个房间，离开这座房子。她不确定罗伯特的话会往哪个方向发展，但是她害怕。她必须离开。她必须在自己陷得更深之前离开。

罗伯特跟着她来到前门。

“嗯，”他说，“我想这就是道别了。再见，基普，再见，劳拉。你什么时候离开？”

“明天，”她说，“那么再见了。谢谢你。”

他把手放在门上。“你没生气吧？你明白我想说什么吗？”

“当然。我们都会对人产生误解。”劳拉说。“我第一次在酒馆里看到你时，我还以为你是一位登山诗人呢。”她说。

他笑了。“嗯，我确实喜欢在山间行走，所以这部分是真的。”他说，“事实上我有时也写诗，所以你并不是全错。”

她笑了。“我得走了。”她说。但是罗伯特的手还放在门上。他一直没开门。

“再见，劳拉。”他又说，她看了看他。她第一次看到他的眼睛正盯着自己的眼睛。

第103页

然后她知道情况发生了。她知道自己无法阻止它。她爱上了这个男人，一个仍旧深爱着已逝女友的男人，一个刚刚和另一个女人走到一起的男人。

第104页

劳拉开车离开罗伯特的房子返回湖泊时，她的眼里泛着泪光。

“发生了什么事？”她纳闷，“这怎么可能发生呢？我是和尼克来的，我却爱上了别人。”

她生气地开着车，一路上雨下得很大。

“通常是我喜欢上一个人，然后发现我不喜欢他们。这次是我遇到一个似乎讨厌我的人，而我发现我喜欢——不，我爱他！罗伯特与尼克太不一样了。他是那么善良，那么体贴！我们的想法也相像……”

她开车时，这些想法一直萦绕在她的脑海里。

“尼克终究不是我想象中的那个人，我不想和他在一起了。罗伯特是我想和他在一起的人。但是我不能！我必须立刻克制住任何感情。”她看着坐在她旁边座位上的基普。“帮帮我，基普，”她说，“帮我忘掉兽医吧！”

第105页

* * *

第二天早上，劳拉和尼克起得很早，准备离开。劳拉又感到不开心了。她怎么可以在那辆小小的车里在尼克身旁再坐六个小时一路返回伦敦呢？很明显，他们彼此已无话可说了。很明显他们俩不合适。

“快点儿！”尼克说，“我不想回去得太晚。我这一周很忙。”

“好的，”劳拉说，“我准备好了。我的包在车里。”她又喊道：“来吧，基普！该回到约瑟夫身边了。”

尼克刚上车，劳拉的手机就响了。劳拉接起了电话。

“喂？”

“劳拉·巴顿吗？”一位女士问。

“是我。”劳拉答道。

“我是圣托马斯医院的护士琼斯。我想您是约瑟夫·唐纳森先生的朋友，对吗？”

“哦，是的。他怎么样了？”劳拉问。

“我很抱歉告诉您，约瑟夫夜里去世了。”护士说。

“什么？”劳拉轻轻地问。

“我很抱歉。我知道这是个噩耗，但他病得很重，他走得很安详。”护士说。

第106页

劳拉想说话，但她唯一能说的就是：“可是他的狗在我这里。”

“对。您能养着它吗？我确信约瑟夫会很乐意由您来养它的。”护士说。

“哦，我从未想过养狗。我有一间小公寓和……”劳拉开始说。她能感觉到眼泪开始顺着她的脸颊滑落。

“不管怎么说，我很抱歉给您带来坏消息。”护士说。

护士说了再见，劳拉默默地坐了一会儿。

“是谁打来的？”尼克问。

“是医院。约瑟夫死了。他们要我照看这只狗。”

“你不能养那只狗！”尼克说，“它已经花掉你一百多英镑了，它不值它惹麻烦花的钱。”

劳拉看着他，她的眼里含着泪水。

“怎么了？”尼克不耐烦地问。

“尼克！我的朋友刚死，可你所能想到的只是这只狗要花我多少钱。”

“我很抱歉。”尼克说，“抱歉，真的。我没考虑到。只是……在你那么小的公寓里你该拿基普怎么办？”

第107页

“我不知道！我没想到会这样。我得想一想。”

劳拉走过谷仓，来到山上，站在那里看着景色，手摸着基普的头，想着约瑟夫。回想他握着自己的手说：“你会照顾它的，对吗？”

基普不知道它的主人已经死了。这似乎太令人伤心。“我该拿你怎么办呢？”她对基普说。

然后，一个主意像一道光芒闪过她的脑际，使得她想要跳起来，想尽可能快地跑下山。

“来，基普！”她说，“我们要再去见见兽医。”

第 16 章 在车站

第108页

“尼克，你介意开车送我和基普到兽医的诊所吗？”她温柔地问道。

“兽医？又是那个兽医？”尼克问。

“是的，尼克，还是那个兽医。我需要问问他是否愿意收养基普。我感觉他们彼此很投缘。”

“好吧，”尼克说，“你这个周末是从兽医的诊所开始的，所以我想在那里结束也挺合适的。”

“之后，可以麻烦你送我去火车站吗？”劳拉说，“我要坐火车回家。我不能和你一起回去了。你知道这一点，不是吗？”

“你在说什么，劳拉？这是因为什么呢？”尼克问。

“看，尼克，我们俩发展得不顺利，对吧？我需要时间思考。”

尼克看着她。“我们的关系结束了吗？”他问。

“你觉得呢？”劳拉说。

“我早该猜到了，”他说，“这就是为什么我通常不会带女人一起度假。从来不灵。”

第109页

“但我们知道不是更好吗？”劳拉说，“我们现在知道而不是用一年的时间才发现我们没有什么共同之处，这不是更好吗?”

“我想这是对的。”尼克说。

有一会儿，劳拉为他感到难过。这事于他是失望，于她亦如此。但他俩都知道她是对的。

* * *

罗伯特低头看着基普。“这么说，”他说，“最终我还是交了一个朋友。”

他几乎要哭了，他不知道这是为什么。他把狗抱起来，它用鼻子碰了碰他的脸颊。

太奇怪了。他现在并不孤单，那为什么他有一种可怕的空虚感，几乎就像基娅拉刚死时那样糟糕呢？他痛苦得想把脸藏在基普的毛里哭泣。

然后他终于想到了。只拥有基普还不够，他还想要劳拉。一想到她已经走了，他再也见不到她了，他就觉得难受。

这是他多久以来第一次有这样的感觉？可是劳拉有尼克，他们今天已经在回去的路上了，回到城市，回到他们喜欢的生活——充满金钱、美酒、服装和其他城里人喜欢的东西。

第110页

* * *

劳拉独自坐在火车站的站台上。尼克把她放在火车站后就开车回伦敦了。她感到孤单。

至少她知道基普已经找到了一个家，是能够找到的最好的家了。约瑟夫会很满意的，她确信这一点。

当火车终于开进车站后，她慢慢上车，希望自己不必离开。

她坐在火车上的一个角落里，回想着刚刚过去的几个小时。罗伯特立即接受了基普，几乎不用请求。

“我当然愿意养它！”他当时说，一抹笑容让他的脸容光焕发。劳拉再次想要吻他，就像第一天晚上他要把基普带回他家时那样。但玛吉在那儿，从门口看着，犹如无声的警告。

劳拉叹了一口气。

火车在两侧的青山之间向南驶去。很快她就会回到城市，回到自己的店。这个周末、美丽的山、罗伯特和基普都将会成为回忆。

第111页

* * *

上午的门诊时间结束后，罗伯特回家吃午饭。房子感觉空荡荡的。罗伯特看着基普，基普疑惑地看着他。

“我又有什么可失去的呢？”他问小狗。

他拿起手机。果然，劳拉的手机号码在上面，在最近给他打过电话的人的名单里。

“劳拉，”她接起电话后他说，“我知道这很疯狂，我知道我听起来疯了。但我只是想再跟你说说话。”有几秒钟的沉默。

“你到家了吗？”他问。

“没有，我没和尼克一起开车回去。我在火车上。我和尼克结束了，我不想跟他一起回去。”

“火车？什么……？下一站是哪里？”罗伯特问。

“奥克森霍尔姆。”劳拉说。

“奥克森霍尔姆？你能在那儿下车吗？下车等我！我去接你。我们需要谈谈。”罗伯特急切地说，“你知道我们之间发生了什么，不是吗？”

“罗伯特，我不能。我得回伦敦。乔期望我明天回到店里。”

第112页

“你可以坐晚一些的火车。求你了。”罗伯特说。

劳拉听着他的声音。她怎么能抗拒呢？

“好吧，”她最后说，“我会在奥克森霍尔姆下车。”

“在火车站等我，”罗伯特说，“我会尽快赶到那儿。”

* * *

劳拉坐在奥克森霍尔姆车站的月台上，感觉有些冷。“我在做什么？”她心想，“我是疯了吗？我明天还要工作。但我需要再见罗伯特一次。而且他想见我！我不可能放下他。”

终于，她抬起头，看到罗伯特和基普朝她走来，她知道她终究是做对了。

罗伯特在月台上跑到她面前，抱住她。

“你一离开，我就知道我不能就这样让你走。”他说，“你能跟我回去吗，就几个小时？你可以搭晚一点儿的火车。”

“但是……但是玛吉会说什么呢？”她问。

“玛吉？我的接待员吗？她会说什么，你问这话是什么意思？”罗伯特问。

“我以为你和她是……我以为……你不是在和她谈恋爱吗？”

第113页

罗伯特抬起头大笑起来。

“抱歉，”他说，“我想不出比这更疯狂的主意了！我喜欢的是你，我需要的是你。我很多年没有这种感觉了。”

劳拉没来得及争辩，就发现自己已经上了路虎车，坐在罗伯特的旁边，驶离车站了。

罗伯特开车沿着小路驶向湖边时，试着不去想两年前的那个晚上。穿过通往湖泊的小树林时，他把手放在基普的头上。他屏住呼吸，等待着它的发生，一直发生的事，可怕的声音、灯光和尖叫声。

他们现在在湖边了。他等待着。什么都没有发生。

他向远处的水面望去。什么都没有，只有午后的阳光柔和地洒在静静的水面上。

四周一片寂静，景色很美。他觉得奇怪，好像比以前轻松了。他觉得自己的胸膛好像装满了东西。

“这是什么呢?”他想，“发生了什么?”

第114页

然后他意识到了。他感到高兴，两年来他第一次感到高兴。

他又伸出手，握住劳拉的手，然后他看着她，她笑了。

“你知道吗，基普吃毒药后你主动提出把它带回家时，”劳拉说，“我就想吻你了。”

“为什么没吻呢?”罗伯特问。

“因为我以为你讨厌我。”她说。

于是他停下路虎车，向她靠近。“现在你可以吻我了。”他说。

他们亲吻时，太阳照亮了他们的脸颊。